CIMA

T4 Part B: Case Study Examination

D PLC – HOUSE BUILDING CASE

CASE ANALYSIS WORKBOOK

CIMA Publishing is an imprint of Elsevier
The Boulevard, Langford Lane, Kidlington, Oxford, OX5 1GB, UK
225 Wyman Street, Waltham, MA 02451, USA
Kaplan Publishing UK, Unit 2 The Business Centre, Molly Millars Lane, Wokingham, Berkshire RG41 2QZ

Notice
No responsibility is assumed by the publisher for any injury and/or damage to persons or property as a matter of products liability, negligence or otherwise, or from any use or operation of any methods, products, instructions or ideas contained in the material herein.

British Library Cataloguing in Publication Data
A catalogue record for this book is available from the British Library

ISBN 978-0-85732-587-7

Printed and bound in Great Britain.

12 13 14 10 9 8 7 6 5 4 3 2 1

Acknowledgements

We are grateful to the Chartered Institute of Management Accountants for permisssion to reproduce the pre-seen material and matrix for the Jot case study. The copyright remains with the examining body.

Contents

		Page
Chapter 1	Kaplan's recommended approach to the Case Study Exam	1
Chapter 2	D plc Pre-seen material and initial thoughts	19
Chapter 3	Strategic and financial analysis of the case material	59
Chapter 4	Ethical considerations	109
Chapter 5	Key issues and options	115
Chapter 6	Prioritising issues	141
Chapter 7	Planning your answer: Mini-case scenarios	155
Chapter 8	Requirement 1(b)	201

Paper Introduction

Overview

The Test of Professional Competence in Management Accounting comprises two component parts that must both be achieved in order to complete the test. Credits are used to ensure success, rather than marks. To pass the Test of Professional Competence in Management Accounting, students must achieve an aggregated minimum of 75 credits – comprising a minimum of 50 credits for Part A (maximum 50 credits) and a minimum of 25 credits for Part B (maximum 50 credits).

Students are advised to undertake Part A and Part B concurrently, although either can be taken in any order once all strategic level examinations have been completed. The overall result for the Test of Professional Competence in Management Accounting can only be given when both component parts have been completed.

T4 Part A – Initial professional development – Work based practical experience

Overview

Students must gain a minimum of three years' relevant work based practical experience. Experience may be drawn from any of the following three areas, but a minimum of 18 months must be gained within the 'Core' area.

Area 1 – Basic experience	Area 2 – Core experience	Area 3 – Supplementary experience
1a. Preparing and maintaining accounting records	2a. Preparation of management accounts	3a. Financial strategy
1b. Statutory and regulatory reporting	2b. Planning, budgeting and forecasting	3b. Corporate finance
1c. IT desktop skills	2c. Management reporting for decision making	3c. Treasury management
1d. Systems and procedure development	2d. Product and service costing	3d. Taxation
	2e. Information management	3e. Business evaluation and appraisal
	2f. Project appraisal	3f. Business strategy
	2g. Project management	3g. External relationships
	2h. Working capital control	
	2i. Risk management and business assurance	

Note: Some or all of the required experience may have been gained before registering as a CIMA student.

Practical experience must be recorded by students within a Career Profile and submitted to CIMA for assessment. An approved Career Profile is awarded 50 credits – the amount needed to meet the requirements for Part A of the Test of Professional Competence in Management Accounting.

Full details of the practical experience requirements and how to complete the CIMA Career Profile can be found on the CIMA website and within a separate publication entitled 'Practical Experience Requirements'. Employers and their students are advised to refer to these documents.

T4 Part B – Case Study Examination

Overview

The examination is based upon a case study that is set within a simulated business context relating to one or more fictitious organisations. However, the context described in the case material is based on a real business or industry.

The examination comprises a three hour assessment of competence, completed within a supervised examination environment. It provides an integrated test of syllabus content that is mainly included within the three strategic level papers – E3, F3 and P3. However, it will also draw upon content covered within the management and operational level papers. The Case Study Examination therefore has no specific syllabus content of its own.

The Case Study Examination primarily involves the application of strategic management accounting techniques to analyse, recommend and support decisions. Students will be required to deal with material in a less structured situation than those encountered in previous strategic level papers, and to integrate a variety of skills to arrive at a recommended solution. It is unlikely that there will be a single right answer to such a complex business problem, and students will be expected to recognise the possible alternatives in dealing with a problem.

The emphasis will be on assessing the student's capabilities and competence in the application of appropriate, relevant knowledge, the ability to demonstrate the higher level skills of synthesis, analysis and evaluation, and skill in effectively presenting and communicating information to users.

Assessment aims

The purpose of the Case Study Examination is to test the capabilities and competence of students, to ensure that they:

A   have a sound technical knowledge of the specific subjects within the curriculum;

B   can apply technical knowledge in an analytical and practical manner;

C   can extract, from various subjects, the knowledge required to solve many-sided or complex problems;

D   can solve a particular problem by distinguishing the relevant information from the irrelevant, in a given body of data;

E   can, in multi-problem situations, identify the problems and prioritise them in the order in which they need to be addressed;

F   appreciate that there can be alternative solutions and understand the role of judgement in dealing with them;

G   can integrate diverse areas of knowledge and skills;

H   can communicate effectively with users, by formulating realistic recommendations in a concise and logical fashion;

I   can identify, advise on and/or resolve ethical dilemmas.

Assessment strategy

There will be a written examination paper of three hours, plus 20 minutes of pre-examination question paper reading time. The paper will have 2 requirements:

- Requirement 1(a) will require the production of a report (and will be worth 90 marks)

- Requirement 1(b) will be a further communication document (and will be worth 10 marks)

The questions will be based upon:

(a) a case study (pre-seen material), which will be published on the CIMA website, at least six weeks in advance of the examination. This will provide an opportunity, before the examination, to undertake preparatory analysis based upon the pre-seen material. The volume of pre-seen material is likely to be between 10 and 20 sides of A4;

(b) further information regarding the case (unseen material), which will be added as part of the examination paper. This will allow further developments to be explained and additional issues to be raised. The volume of unseen material is likely to be between three and six sides of A4 paper.

Questions will test the students' capabilities and competence in the application of appropriate knowledge, and the processes undertaken in dealing with the problems identified in the examination, together with the ability to present and communicate information in a variety of formats. The pre-seen material will also contain details of the Assessment Criteria showing the scoring system to be used when assessing the capabilities and competence of candidates.

To successfully pass Part B of the Test of Professional Competence in Management Accounting – Case Study Examination, students must score a minimum of 25 credits (out of a possible maximum of 50 credits).

Learning outcomes

Students will be required to go through the following stages to prepare for, and to answer, the requirements of the Case Study Examination:

A – Preparatory to the exam

- analyse the context within which the case is set;
- analyse the current position of the organisation;
- identify and analyse the issues facing the organisation.

Note: These activities will be undertaken using the published 'pre-seen' case study material.

B – During the exam

- analyse the current position of the organisation;
- identify, analyse and prioritise the issues facing the organisation;
- identify, evaluate and discuss possible feasible options / courses of action available;
- recommend and justify a course of action;
- prepare and present information in a report format and to a standard suitable for presentation to senior management as specified in the question requirement;
- prepare and present a further communication document in a format as specified in the question requirement.

Note: These activities will be undertaken using the 'pre-seen' and 'unseen' case study materials.

How to Use the Materials

This Kaplan Publishing T4 Case Study Examination: Case Analysis Workbook has been written for the **D plc House-Building** case study examination. It provides an analysis of the pre-seen material for the students sitting the T4 Case Study Exam as well as additional guidance and tips on exam technique.

To be successful, you need a good understanding of the pre-seen material before you attempt the exam as there will not be enough time in the exam itself for thinking about issues and carrying out analysis that you should have done already. This workbook will help you fully analyse the pre-seen material to ensure you are well prepared on the day.

It contains the following:

- Initial thoughts on the pre-seen material with suggestions on areas where more detailed analysis might be required.

- Detailed analysis of the pre-seen information through the application of strategic models and financial analysis: looks at the data given in the pre-seen from different perspectives (enterprise strategy, financial strategy, performance strategy), using the knowledge and skills gained from the Strategic Level papers.

- Ethical considerations: takes you through some of the ethical issues seen within the pre-seen material.

- Identification of key issues and options available for the company.

- Summary of the case: takes you through a short clear summary of the essential facts to help you absorb and understand the data.

- Prioritisation exercises: a chance to practise the process of prioritisation with some potential endings that could arise in the exam.

- Mini case scenarios: using some brief possible scenarios, you can test your knowledge of the critical areas of the business as well as practising the processes you will need to follow when sitting a full exam. The scenarios will draw on a number of different thinking techniques, thereby equipping you for a range of different issues you could be faced with in the exam. These scenarios will also help to prepare you before your sit your first practice exam. Some of these mini-scenarios are also developed into requirement 1 (b)s allowing you to practise this area of the exam as well.

We provide you with feedback and suggested answers to all questions and practice exercises.

In addition to this workbook, you will also have access to additional online resources via **EN-gage**. At the front of this book you will find information on how to access these FREE online resources, which include:

- Recap tests

  These should be used before you start studying to help identify any weaknesses in your under-pinning knowledge.

- Case Analysis Recording

  After reading the pre-seen material for the first time, you should watch the Case Analysis Recording. This will help develop your familiarisation with the material and encourage you to start thinking about the information from different perspectives.

How to prepare for the T4 Case Study Exam

In order to adequately prepare for the T4 Case Study Exam, we would recommend you undertake the following:

- Ensure you have a solid understanding of technical models and financial analysis techniques

  Use the recap tests found on EN-gage to check for weak areas. Where you get a question wrong, ensure you spend some time re-visiting the concepts being tested.

- Develop an understanding of the Case Study Pre-seen material and the challenges posed in the industry setting.

  Follow the guidance laid out in chapter 1 of this workbook to ensure you become approach the pre-seen in the most efficient way.

- Ensure you are familiar with the Case Study Assessment Criteria and top-tips for how to tackle the exam itself.

  Use the information in this workbook as well as the many articles on the CIMA website to develop your awareness of the best approaches.

- Practise using mock exams.

  There is simply no substitute for completing practice exams under time pressure. Try to do as many as you can and evaluate your answer carefully to identify areas for improvement.

Icon Explanations

 Key Point - identifies elements which are key to this case.

 Practice exercises - a core part of the analysis process are exercises which give you the opportunity to test your understanding of key areas. Within the work book the answers to these sections are left blank, answers to the questions can be found at the back of each chapter or within the online version which can be hidden or shown on screen to enable repetition of activities.

 Exclamation Mark - this symbol signifies an area which can be more difficult to understand, when reviewing these areas care should be taken.

 Expandable Text - a more detailed explanation of key terms or theories; these sections will help to provide a deeper understanding on areas previously covered within your CIMA studies.

APPLICABLE MATHS TABLES AND FORMULAE

Present value table

Present value of £1 i.e. $(1 + r)^{-n}$ where r = interest rate, n = number of periods until payment or receipt.

Periods (n)	Interest rates (r)									
	1%	2%	3%	4%	5%	6%	7%	8%	9%	10%
1	.990	.980	.971	.962	.962	.943	.935	.926	.917	.909
2	.980	.961	.943	.925	.907	.890	.873	.857	.842	.826
3	.971	.942	.915	.889	.864	.840	.816	.794	.772	.751
4	.961	.924	.888	.855	.823	.792	.763	.735	.708	.683
5	.951	.906	.863	.822	.784	.747	.713	.681	.650	.621
6	.942	.888	.837	.790	.746	.705	.666	.630	.596	.564
7	.933	.871	.813	.760	.711	.665	.623	.583	.547	.513
8	.923	.853	.789	.731	.677	.627	.582	.540	.502	.467
9	.914	.837	.766	.703	.645	.592	.544	.500	.460	.424
10	.905	.820	.744	.676	.614	.558	.508	.463	.422	.386
11	.896	.804	.722	.650	.585	.527	.475	.429	.388	.350
12	.887	.788	.701	.625	.557	.497	.444	.397	.356	.319
13	.879	.773	.681	.601	.530	.469	.415	.368	.326	.290
14	.870	.758	.661	.577	.505	.442	.388	.340	.299	.263
15	.861	.743	.642	.555	.481	.417	.362	.315	.275	.239
16	.853	.728	.623	.534	.458	.394	.339	.292	.252	.218
17	.844	.714	.605	.513	.436	.371	.317	.270	.231	.198
18	.836	.700	.587	.494	.416	.350	.296	.250	.212	.180
19	.828	.686	.570	.475	.396	.331	.277	.232	.194	.164
20	.820	.673	.554	.456	.377	.312	.258	.215	.178	.149

Periods (n)	Interest rates (r)									
	11%	12%	13%	14%	15%	16%	17%	18%	19%	20%
1	.901	.893	.885	.877	.870	.862	.855	.847	.840	.833
2	.812	.797	.783	.769	.756	.743	.731	.718	.706	.694
3	.731	.712	.693	.675	.658	.641	.624	.609	.593	.579
4	.659	.636	.613	.592	.572	.552	.534	.516	.499	.482
5	.593	.567	.543	.519	.497	.476	.456	.437	.419	.402
6	.535	.507	.480	.456	.432	.410	.390	.370	.352	.335
7	.482	.452	.425	.400	.376	.354	.333	.314	.296	.279
8	.434	.404	.376	.351	.327	.305	.285	.266	.249	.233
9	.391	.361	.333	.308	.284	.263	.243	.225	.209	.194
10	.352	.322	.295	.270	.247	.227	.208	.191	.176	.162
11	.317	.287	.261	.237	.215	.195	.178	.162	.148	.135
12	.286	.257	.231	.208	.187	.168	.152	.137	.124	.112
13	.258	.229	.204	.182	.163	.145	.130	.116	.104	.093
14	.232	.205	.181	.160	.141	.125	.111	.099	.088	.078
15	.209	.183	.160	.140	.123	.108	.095	.084	.074	.065
16	.188	.163	.141	.123	.107	.093	.081	.071	.062	.054
17	.170	.146	.125	.108	.093	.080	.069	.060	.052	.045
18	.153	.130	.111	.095	.081	.069	.059	.051	.044	.038
19	.138	.116	.098	.083	.070	.060	.051	.043	.037	.031
20	.124	.104	.087	.073	.061	.051	.043	.037	.031	.026

Cumulative present value of 1.00 unit of currency per annum, receivable or payable at the end of each year for n years $\dfrac{1-(1+r)^{-n}}{r}$.

Periods (n)	Interest rates (r)									
	1%	2%	3%	4%	5%	6%	7%	8%	9%	10%
1	0.990	0.980	0.971	0.962	0.952	0.943	0.935	0.926	0.917	0.909
2	1.970	1.942	1.913	1.886	1.859	1.833	1.808	1.783	1.759	1.736
3	2.941	2.884	2.829	2.775	2.723	2.673	2.624	2.577	2.531	2.487
4	3.902	3.808	3.717	3.630	3.546	3.465	3.387	3.312	3.240	3.170
5	4.853	4.713	4.580	4.452	4.329	4.212	4.100	3.993	3.890	3.791
6	5.795	5.601	5.417	5.242	5.076	4.917	4.767	4.623	4.486	4.355
7	6.728	6.472	6.230	6.002	5.786	5.582	5.389	5.206	5.033	4.868
8	7.652	7.325	7.020	6.733	6.463	6.210	5.971	5.747	5.535	5.335
9	8.566	8.162	7.786	7.435	7.108	6.802	6.515	6.247	5.995	5.759
10	9.471	8.983	8.530	8.111	7.722	7.360	7.024	6.710	6.418	6.145
11	10.368	9.787	9.253	8.760	8.306	7.887	7.499	7.139	6.805	8.495
12	11.255	10.575	9.954	9.385	8.863	8.384	7.943	7.536	7.161	6.814
13	12.134	11.348	10.635	9.986	9.394	8.853	8.358	7.904	7.487	7.103
14	13.004	12.106	11.296	10.563	9.899	9.295	8.745	8.244	7.786	7.367
15	13.865	12.849	11.938	11.118	10.380	9.712	9.108	8.559	8.061	7.606
16	14.718	13.578	12.561	11.652	10.838	10.106	9.447	8.851	8.313	7.824
17	15.562	14.292	13.166	12.166	11.274	10.477	9.763	9.122	8.544	8.022
18	16.398	14.992	13.754	12.659	11.690	10.828	10.059	9.372	8.756	8.201
19	17.226	15.679	14.324	13.134	12.085	11.158	10.336	9.604	8.950	8.365
20	18.046	16.351	14.878	13.590	12.462	11.470	10.594	9.818	9.129	8.514

Periods (n)	Interest rates (r)									
	11%	12%	13%	14%	15%	16%	17%	18%	19%	20%
1	0.901	0.893	0.885	0.877	0.870	0.862	0.685	0.847	0.840	0.833
2	1.713	1.690	1.668	1.647	1.626	1.605	1.585	1.566	1.547	1.528
3	2.444	2.402	2.361	2.322	2.283	2.246	2.210	2.174	2.140	2.106
4	3.102	3.037	2.974	2.914	2.855	2.798	2.743	2.690	2.639	2.589
5	3.696	3.605	3.517	3.433	3.352	3.274	3.199	3.127	3.058	2.991
6	4.231	4.111	3.998	3.889	3.784	3.685	3.589	3.498	3.410	3.326
7	4.712	4.564	4.423	4.288	4.160	4.039	3.922	3.812	3.706	3.605
8	5.146	4.968	4.799	4.639	4.487	4.344	4.207	4.078	3.954	3.837
9	5.537	5.328	5.132	4.946	4.772	4.607	4.451	4.303	4.163	4.031
10	5.889	5.650	5.426	5.216	5.019	4.833	4.659	4.494	4.339	4.192
11	6.207	5.938	5.687	5.453	5.234	5.029	4.836	4.656	4.486	4.327
12	6.492	6.194	5.918	5.660	5.421	5.197	4.968	4.793	4.611	4.439
13	6.750	6.424	6.122	5.842	5.583	5.342	5.118	4.910	4.715	4.533
14	6.982	6.628	6.302	6.002	5.724	5.468	5.229	5.008	4.802	4.611
15	7.191	6.811	6.462	6.142	5.847	5.575	5.324	5.092	4.876	4.675
16	7.379	6.974	6.604	6.265	5.954	5.668	5.405	5.162	4.938	4.730
17	7.549	7.120	6.729	6.373	6.047	5.749	5.475	5.222	4.990	4.775
18	7.702	7.250	6.840	6.467	6.128	5.818	5.534	5.273	5.033	4.812
19	7.839	7.366	6.938	6.550	6.198	5.877	5.584	5.316	5.070	4.843
20	7.963	7.469	7.025	6.623	6.259	5.929	5.628	5.353	5.101	4.870

FORMULAE

Valuation Models

(i) Irredeemable preference share, paying a constant annual dividend, d, in perpetuity, where P_0 is the ex-div value:

$$P_0 = \frac{d}{k_{pref}}$$

(ii) Ordinary (Equity) share, paying a constant annual dividend, d, in perpetuity, where P_0 is the ex-div value:

$$P_0 = \frac{d}{k_e}$$

(iii) Ordinary (Equity) share, paying an annual dividend, d, growing in perpetuity at a constant rate, g, where P_0 is the ex-div value:

$$P_0 = \frac{d_1}{k_e - g} \quad \text{or} \quad P_0 = \frac{d_0[1+g]}{k_e - g}$$

(iv) Irredeemable (Undated) debt, paying annual after tax interest, i(1 – t), in perpetuity, where P_0 is the ex-interest value:

$$P_0 = \frac{i[1-t]}{k_{d\ net}}$$

or, without tax:

$$P_0 = \frac{i}{k_d}$$

(v) Future value of S, of a sum X, invested for n periods, compounded at r% interest:

$$S = X[1+r]^n$$

(vi) Present value of £1 payable or receivable in n years, discounted at r% per annum:

$$PV = \frac{1}{[1+r]^n}$$

(vii) Present value of an annuity of £1 per annum, receivable or payable for n years, commencing in one year, discounted at r% per annum:

$$PV = \frac{1}{r}\left[1 - \frac{1}{[1+r]^n}\right]$$

(viii) Present value of £1 per annum, payable or receivable in perpetuity, commencing in one year, discounted at r% per annum:

$$PV = \frac{1}{r}$$

(ix) Present value of £1 per annum, receivable or payable, commencing in one year, growing in perpetuity at a constant rate of g% per annum, discounted at r% per annum:

$$PV = \frac{1}{r-g}$$

Cost of Capital

(i) Cost of irredeemable preference capital, paying an annual dividend d in perpetuity, and having a current ex-div price P_0:

$$k_{pref} = \frac{d}{P_0}$$

(ii) Cost of irredeemable debt capital, paying annual net interest i(1 – t), and having a current ex-interest price P0:

$$k_{d\ net} = \frac{i[1-t]}{P_0}$$

(iii) Cost of ordinary (equity) share capital, paying an annual dividend d in perpetuity, and having a current ex-div price P_0:

$$k_e = \frac{d}{P_0}$$

(iv) Cost of ordinary (equity) share capital, having a current ex-div price, P_0, having just paid a dividend, d_0, with the dividend growing in perpetuity by a constant g% per annum:

$$k_e = \frac{d_1}{P_0} + g \quad \text{or} \quad k_e = \frac{d_0[1+g]}{P_0} + g$$

(v) Cost of ordinary (equity) share capital, using the CAPM:

$$k_e = R_f + \left[R_m - R_f\right]\beta$$

(vi) Weighted average cost of capital, k_0:

$$k_0 = k_{eg}\left[\frac{V_E}{V_E + V_D}\right] + k_d\left[\frac{V_D}{V_E + V_D}\right]$$

Kaplan's recommended approach to the Case Study Exam

Chapter learning objectives

By the end of this chapter you will:

- Be clear about Kaplan's recommended approach to analysing and understanding the pre-seen material.

- Understand how best to use the Case Analysis Recording available on EN-gage.

- Know which websites might help you gain a better understanding of the current case study.

- Be aware of some recent comments made by the examiner.

- Know about good techniques to adopt in the exam (including report layout and time management).

1 Exam background

Assessment strategy

The Test of Professional Competence provides a final test and can be taken only after all the Strategic Level subjects have been successfully completed.

There is a written examination paper of 3 hours (plus an extra 20 minutes' reading time). You will be asked to prepare a report together with a smaller communication document such as a presentation, e-mail or letter.

The exam will test your capabilities and competence in the application of appropriate knowledge and the processes undertaken in dealing with the problems identified in the exam, together with your ability to present and communicate information.

Introduction to the pre-seen material

The pre-seen material consists of 11 pages of text together with appendices containing financial and other data. On the day of the exam, you will receive a slightly larger booklet containing the same pre-seen material but with additional pages of unseen material. You will also be given instructions about what you are required to do.

You cannot take into the exam room your annotated copy of the pre-seen material or any other notes. When the exam starts, you are therefore required to start all over again, but with additional unseen material to read.

However, studying the pre-seen thoroughly before the exam day will help you because:

- Reading the pre-seen material carefully and analysing it thoroughly will make you more familiar with its content and layout. This will save you a lot of time in the exam and make you much better prepared.

- You will need to apply many of the same skills to analyse the unseen material in the exam as you need for analysing the pre-seen. Working on the pre-seen material is therefore excellent practice.

- You will need to have ideas about how you might analyse the numbers in the pre-seen material, because you could find yourself wanting to make the same type of calculation in the exam itself.

2 Familiarisation with pre-seen material

Familiarisation with the pre-seen material and the industry in which the organisation operates will underpin your ability to assess the impact of the issues presented in the unseen material. It will also equip you to identify and evaluate alternative courses of action.

The best approach to familiarising yourself with the material can be summarised as:

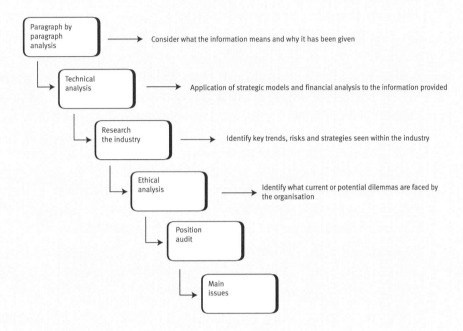

To complete this process we recommend that you:

- **Read the pre-seen material from beginning to end without making any notes**, simply to familiarise yourself with the scenario. Read the material again, as many times as you think necessary, without making notes. You can do this over a period of several days, if you wish. When you think you are reasonably familiar with the situation described by the material, you should start to make notes.

- **Start to make notes**. By making notes, you will become more familiar with the detail of the scenario. We recommend that you make notes on each paragraph (or each group of short paragraphs) in the pre-seen material. Think about what the paragraph is telling you, and consider how this information might be of interest or relevance.

- **Listen to the case analysis recording.** A brief analysis of the case, recorded by an expert Kaplan tutor, can be found on Kaplan EN-gage. This should not act as a substitute for performing your own review but should be used to supplement your own processes to ensure you consider the material from a number of different angles.

- **Do some simple calculations**. You are given some figures in the pre-seen material. Do some simple calculations, such as margin analysis, ROCE, company valuations, working capital ratios etc as these might give you a picture of changes over time. Refer to chapter three for more on this.

- **Revise any 'technical' topics that might be relevant**. If you have forgotten about topics that come up in the pre-seen material, go back to your previous study materials and revise them.

- **Use one or more 'formal' techniques to analyse the pre-seen material**, using your notes and your background understanding of the industry. The aim of this analysis is to identify, if possible, the position and prospects of the organisation in the case study. Chapter 3 of this workbook will help you with this.

- **Find out what you can about the industry in which the case study organisation operates.** Carry out some research into the industry in which the organisation described in the case study operates. You can use a search engine such as Google® or Yahoo® to find information on the Internet or you can access specially prepared industry briefing documents such as that prepared by Kaplan. You can also identify one or more companies that actually operate in the industry, and visit their websites and find out what you can about them. Use our 'Useful websites' section to get you started.

- **Ethical analysis.** Consider any ethical issues highlighted within the pre-seen material. Make sure you're clear about the ethical dimension and consider what actions could be taken.

- **Summarise your analysis**. Prepare a position audit and identify a list of the main issues facing the company at present. From this you should identify those factors that will drive your prioritisations in the exam.

- **Give yourself more time to think**. Spend as much time as you can thinking about the case study. You don't have to be sitting at a desk to do this. You can think about the case study when you travel to work or in any spare time that you have for thinking.
    - When new ideas come to you, jot them down.
    - If you think of a new approach to financial analysis, carry out any calculations you feel might be useful.

Never forget that this exam is not really testing what you have learned. It is testing your ability to analyse, assess, evaluate and apply judgement to 'realistic' business problems and new opportunities and proposals. Thinking about the case study allows you to exercise these abilities. We therefore recommend very strongly that you allow yourself as much time as possible for the thinking process.

Just before the exam, you should go over the pre-seen material and your notes again. Compare your earlier thoughts about the case study with your current thinking, which may well have changed. Make sure that your ideas are still consistent with the information in the pre-seen material.

Industry research - Useful websites

In addition to becoming familiar with the pre-seen material, it important that you perform some external research in order to understand the challenges posed in the industry setting. This research should include some industry-specific aspects as well as broader research on current business and economic issues.

Within the assessment criteria, there are five specific 'diversity' marks, awarded for bring in real-life examples to support your analysis of the issues in the exam. More widely, a good understanding of the industry will also help you pick up prioritisation, focus, judgement and logic marks, as all are linked to sound commercial reasoning. The better your understanding of the industry and the economy in which it operates, the better your commercial reasoning will be.

The following are some suggested useful websites that may help with this research.

Search engines

www.google.com
www.msn.co.uk
www.yahoo.com

General

www.bbc.co.uk
www.ft.com
www.economist.com

Industry / topic specific

http://about.taylorwimpey.co.uk
http://www.barrattdevelopments.co.uk
http://corporate.persimmonhomes.com
http://www.guardian.co.uk/business/construction

3 Examiner's comments

It is useful to look at the comments of the chief examiner on the performance of candidates in previous exam sittings. These can be found in the Post Exam Guidance document written after each sitting, all of which can be found on CIMA's website. Problems that the examiner identifies in one exam often re-appear in every exam.

A selection of past comments are set out below.

Using the assessment criteria

Remember that the assessment criteria give you some guidance about what you should be doing in your answer to earn as many marks as possible. Look at where the marks will be awarded, and plan your answer accordingly.

The following guidance from CIMA is typical:

'There are clear signs that many candidates are responding in appropriate ways to the challenge of a new type of examination, planning the report to cover all indicated sub-requirements and with due regard for the requirements of the marking matrix.'

Answering the question set

Note that the above comment also stresses the importance of answering all elements of the question. Failing to answer the entire question that has been set could be disastrous!

Our recommendation is that you should analyse the pre-seen material as thoroughly as you can but, if you try to forecast what the unseen material will look like, make sure that in the exam you answer the actual question rather than the one you anticipated, addressing only the issues the exam requirement asks you to.

A comment from the examiner has been:

'There was a significant problem with some candidates who had placed too much reliance on their forecasting of the likely question rather than dealing with the quite specific requirement.'

Preparing with mock exams

This workbook is designed to enable you to prepare for the exam by practising on mini unseens and completing prioritisation exercises, in addition to analysing the pre-seen material. However, it is also important that you attempt at least one mock exam, under timed conditions, before sitting the real exam. The post-exam guidance has stated:

'Most candidates ... have learned how to handle the examination by the basic preparation of trying a mock examination.'

Kaplan write a number of mock exams for each case study, and these are available to those who book onto a Kaplan course.

Give reasons for your recommendations

When the question asks you to give recommendations, make sure that you give clear reasons for the recommendations you decide to give.

'There was a problem with candidates providing sensible recommendations but making little effort to provide appropriate reasons for these recommendations ... Candidates should read a requirement for recommendations as implying recommendations with reasons.'

However, it might be reasonable to make a recommendation by referring to previous arguments put forward in your report. Marks are allowed where it is clear from the previous analysis why certain courses of action are being recommended. A good approach to ensure you cover everything is to use sub-headings of 'Recommendation', 'Justification' and 'Actions' when writing your recommendations section of your report.

Another mistake to avoid is making only hesitant suggestions on the grounds that 'we need more information' or 'we need more accurate information'. Although this comment might be valid up to a point, recommendations in 'real life' are based on incomplete and imperfect information, and the case study tries to mirror real life.

Finally, you must ensure that all recommendations are commercially realistic in order to gain good marks.

Calculations

Make sure that you provide a suitable amount of calculations and set out your workings clearly. Calculations with workings can often be presented as an appendix to the report required by the question. It has been surprising how often the post-exam guidance has made comments such as:

'The quality of calculations was generally disappointing.'

Allocate your time in the examination

It is a long-standing rule for candidates that time during the exam should be allocated sensibly between the tasks that the candidate is required to perform. Unfortunately, a number of candidates always fall into the trap of spending too much time preparing the case study answer, and not enough time on the formal answer. A typical comment from CIMA is:

'A number of candidates have clearly spent far too much time on the preliminaries and too little time on the required report.'

Summary of other frequently made comments

Below is a summary of other areas often flagged by the examiner, together with recommendations of what to do, and what not to do.

Stage of exam process	Marks gained by	Marks missed by
Analysis of pre-seen material	Conducting own effective analysis of pre-seen material: • using financial analysis on the data in the pre-seen material • applying strategic models and analysis to see the bigger picture of the strategic position of the company • recognising organisational issues in the case. Bringing relevant aspects of the pre-seen material into the final report.	Relying on third party published analysis: • which candidates could not repeat in the exam room • which did not take account of the changes introduced in the unseen material • which they did not understand or could not argue convincingly in their reports. Failing to take pre-seen data into account in the final report due to lack of familiarity.
	Recognising which technical skills or knowledge may be required in the exam and revising them.	Failing to look beneath the surface of the material and considering the strategic position of the business. Failing to spot obvious strategic, organisational or financial issues in the pre-seen material. Reporting analysis of the pre-seen in the exam rather than answering the requirement (s) set.

Stage of exam process	Marks gained by	Marks missed by
Familiarisation with industry	Researching of the industry background adequately. Appropriately using real-world examples and terminology to support arguments in the final report. Recognising the critical success factors and risks of the industry from the experience of real companies.	Seeking to identify 'real-world' companies and confusing their future course with the future course of the case study. Over-exploring technological and business issues that subsequently clutter the final report. Spending too much time on industry research in preference to other crucial activities like analysing the pre-seen material, practising numerical skills and completing simulations against the clock.
Synthesis of findings	Achieving a high standard of analysis. Forecasting and practising the skills likely to be called for on the exam day. Provisionally prioritising the issues facing the company from information in the pre-seen material. Recognising the mark weightings available in the pre-published assessment matrix.	Failing to update this view in the light of data in the unseen material.

Stage of exam process	Marks gained by	Marks missed by
Exam day techniques	Clearly prioritising major before minor issues. Using recognised analysis models to spot issues and to back up arguments in the report, and including these as appendices. Appropriately allocating time in a time-pressured exam between: • preliminary analysis of the unseen material • answer planning • calculations • writing the report required. Providing sensible advice to management with recommendations being subject to certain conditions, if appropriate. Using appendices for calculations, including explanations with key summary figures brought back into the body of the report.	Failing to take into account numerical and other data from the unseen material. Failing to synthesise the entire case by utilising both the pre-seen and unseen material. Failing to spot or discuss major issues or problems in the case or problems associated with recommendations being made. Failing to complete calculations and so: • failing to get marks for both numerical skills and depth • failing to gain a complete understanding. Spending too long on preliminaries (introductions, terms of reference) and conclusions. Not providing firm recommendations. Not providing reasons for recommendations. Leaving good numerical analysis buried in the appendix rather than bringing it into the argument of the report.

It's worth remembering that if you're sitting the exam in May or November, the Post Exam Guidance document relating to the first sitting of your case study (in either March or August) will usually be available before the second sitting. This should be viewed as essential reading in order to prepare for your exam.

4 Exam technique

Introduction

Success or failure on T4, regardless of whether you sit it as a paper- or computer-based exam, depends on what you can produce in 3 hours under exam conditions. What you have to do is:

- Complete your work in the time available. Don't produce an incomplete report, or a report that you have to rush to finish.

- Produce a paper that satisfies the examiner that you have demonstrated a sufficient level of skills, as set out in the assessment matrix.

Computer-based exam

The idea behind doing the T4 case study exam on a computer is to make it feel more like a day at work. While the skills required to produce a good analysis and report on a PC are slightly different, the basic principles of the computer exam are the same as for the conventional exam. Your computer skills are not being tested, and no credit (or penalty) will be applied to them – the computer is just a vehicle to allow you to produce a more professional report. The skills that are being assessed are those defined by the assessment criteria.

Using a PC to produce your answer

The main software packages that you will be using in the exam are Word® (word processing) and Excel® (spreadsheet). Make sure that you are familiar with the features and functions of these packages, and use the tuition phase of your course to practise (including practising preparing graphs in Excel for a possible part (b) requirement). In the exam, don't try to do anything new; just stick to the basic functions and you will reduce the risk of any problem arising.

It is possible that the examiner may ask for a brief presentation as part of the exam requirements. If so, construct your slides within the Word document. You will not be expected to use PowerPoint® for this task.

Avoid 'linking' worksheets to reports, as this makes file management complicated and increases the risk of losing your work. Just do your detailed calculations in the spreadsheet workbook, and quote the 'bottom line' figures in the report. There is no need to reproduce (or copy) spreadsheet calculations from the Excel workbook to the Word report. The marker will be happy to look at your spreadsheet appendices.

Make sure that in both Word and Excel, you switch on the 'auto-recover' options and set them to a relatively short time period (say, 3 or 4 minutes). Also, select the option to 'create backup copies automatically' as this will ensure that you always have two versions of your work. In Excel, the auto-recover feature is an 'add-in' in some versions, so you need to install it (from the 'tools, add-ins' feature on the menu bar) before it appears in the 'tools' menu. Note: Your tutor or exam invigilator will most probably have already set these options on your PC – check with them before you start the exam.

Answer plan

Doing an answer plan in Word is really easy. This is what we suggest you do:

- Create a contents page, change things around until you are happy with the report structure, then save it.
- Now, copy the contents page, and paste it onto the next page.
- At the beginning of each line on your 'second' contents page, insert a page break.
- You are now left with a section heading at the top of each page, and you can start to complete your report.

Try to design each worksheet so it can be viewed on the screen without scrolling. This makes it less likely that the marker will miss any of your calculations.

Rename any worksheets, and delete any that you don't use.

If you are doing a series of comparisons (for example, a number of NPV calculations) do each on a separate worksheet, then have a summary sheet that shows the results side-by-side.

Don't use the NPV formulae (or any other complex formulae) in Excel. They are difficult to get right, and easy to get wrong. You will tend to trust the results are correct, rather than checking them. Instead, lay out your DCF, and other calculations, the way you would on paper. They are much easier to read (and to mark) that way.

Don't forget to show all your workings and to label calculations so it is obvious what they are (see 'Footnotes and comments', below). The marker will give you credit for the parts of calculations that are correct, so make their life easy.

Selective use of borders and colour can make your worksheets more understandable, but don't go over the top.

Report layout

Use a very basic and simple font, such as Arial or Times New Roman, in an appropriate size. This makes your report look very professional and easy to read. Avoid elaborate fonts.

As with any report, use a cover page and clear headings and sub-headings to separate your work. Starting each section of your report on a new page makes it easier to read.

Don't bother re-typing calculations into a report appendix. Just put 'see Excel workbook' in the appendix.

Note: The blank file that you will have on your PC, within which to create your report, will have a pre-set header (showing your candidate number) and a pre-set footer (showing the page number). Your report cover page will be page 1. Do not change these headers and footers.

Footnotes and comments

In Word, you can use 'insert, footnote' to do just that. This is useful for cross-referencing to appendices or referencing authors. In both Word and Excel, you can use 'insert, comment' to put notes to clarify any complex aspects of your report or calculations.

Paper-based exam

In the exam room you will be given two answer books.

We suggest that you should organise yourself as follows.

- Keep the first answer book free for writing the main body of your report.

- Turn to the middle of the second book (the pages with the staples) and then turn one page further towards the back. The first half of this book is for your appendices and the second half is for planning and rough working. When you assemble your final script at the end of the exam you can have your report in one book and your appendices easily available for the marker to refer to.

- Turn to the first double page spread in the rough workings section at the back of your second answer book (i.e. the double page spread immediately following the pages with the staples).

- Divide the pages equally between the questions or sections of the requirement, adding an extra three sections for introduction, conclusions and recommendations.

- Write the headings of the subsections of the document.

Under each subsection write bullet points describing what you will cover in that section. For any numerical calculations, you can do your workings if you have time (and then present them more neatly in an appendix).

Time management in the exam

Your ability to answer the question set will not only require a sound knowledge and good technique; it will require a disciplined management of your time in the exam. A suggested starting point would be:

Stage	Action	Time
Reading	Initial read through and decision on top 4 issues	20 mins
Planning your answer	Consideration of impact / alternative solutions and content for secondary requirement	20 mins
Appendices	Preparation of SWOT analysis and all numerical appendices	25 mins
Prioritisation statement	Write the prioritisation section of your report	10 mins
Ethics	Write the ethical issues section of your report	15 mins
Key issue (1)	Write the analysis of the issue(s) to which the second requirement relates, followed immediately by writing the recommendation (20 mins in total split approximately 50:50 between analysis and recommendations)	20 mins
Requirement 1(b)	Write your answer to part (b) of the requirement	15 mins
Remaining key issues	Cover the remaining issues (for each one write the analysis followed immediately by writing the recommendation (20 mins per issue × 3 issues)	60 mins
Tidy up	Write your introduction, terms of reference and conclusion, read / spell check your report	15 mins

Sections in a report

The likelihood is that you will have to prepare a report as your answer. Reports should have a clear structure and format. Typically, a report will contain:

- **Title data**: title of the report (brief and descriptive), recipient, date, author and its status (e.g. confidential).

- **Contents page**: a list of contents with each main section and a list of appendices.

- **Introduction**: three short paragraphs covering performance to date, future prospects and key issues facing the company.

- **Terms of reference**: this may contain a brief statement of the purpose of the report (who asked for it and why, who did the work), plus any disclaimers.

- **Identification of key issues**: key issues should be identified and your prioritisation explained.

- **Main body of the report – evaluations/development**: develop the argument or analysis in a logical order, possibly dealing with a number of issues, one at a time and in turn. Make sure that this part of the report meets the requirements of the 'question'. The arguments you put forward in this part of the report should lead on to your recommendations and conclusions. This part of your report should contain the storyline, identify key issues, analyse results, give alternative courses of action, show pros and cons for each, state why some are rejected and, if feasible, rank in order (best first) .

- **Ethical considerations**: for each ethical issue identified discuss why it is an ethical issue, and the possible implications if it is allowed to continue. Follow this with clear advice on the actions to be taken along with justification for each piece of advice.

- **Recommendations**: the next steps that you advise the recipient to take – action (or no action) recommended as a result of the conclusions reached. Include a timescale for completion of major areas. If asked for a recommendation, give one – it shows you could make the decision yourself.

- **Conclusion**: a summary of (logic of/balance of) the arguments and reservations, missing information, further work needed.

- **Appendices**: a place for numerical tables and calculations and any special diagrams (e.g. SWOT chart). All financial data prepared in the appendices should be discussed in the main body of the report.

A report does not contain the items singled out by the examiner for criticism:

- an executive summary
- separate flyleaf pages between the sections.

The report should have an argument

The examiner has repeatedly said that the case study requirement could simply be read as 'advise management'. Therefore a report that doesn't provide 'advice' is going to fail; your report must have an argument.

The argument (and advice) should be made clear in the introduction.

The rest of the report must justify your advice by showing how you came to your conclusion. If you refer to an appendix, make sure that the information you are presenting is clear and relates to the argument you are putting forward.

The conclusion should be brief and merely confirm the argument.

Your recommendations should advise management what to do next.

It is vital that you decide your argument before you write out your skeleton plan (and certainly before you try to write your report).

The plan shows you what to write in your final report

Once your skeleton plan is complete, you have answered the case study. This process should take about an hour of exam room time (including the preparation of your numerical analysis). This leaves you two hours to write the report. Running out of time should not be a problem because your plan will save you wasting time writing about things that distract your reader from the argument and do not gain marks.

Deciding your argument

You need to 'take a view' about what you will recommend. Candidates find this the hardest thing to do in practice and often fail the exam by producing a meandering report that doesn't address the requirement and doesn't come to any clear conclusions on what management should do.

Common causes of problems seem to be:

- Being scared of recommending the wrong thing and failing the exam; you need to be decisive and make clear recommendations with justification as to why you think the company should take this action.

- Providing flawed recommendations based on incorrect financial analysis, such as rejecting a new proposal which your incorrect calculations showed to have a negative NPV when it was financially viable.

- Failing to show enough analysis of all the case material and providing enough business knowledge.

- Getting so wound up in the preparatory analysis and evaluations of pros and cons that no clear conclusion emerges. The candidate writes a report that just goes round in circles.

There is no need for this.

- The examiner doesn't insist that you come to the same conclusion that he/she might have. Just ensure you justify your own conclusion and you will get the marks.

- In supporting your argument you will have ample chance to show your skills of analysis. Besides, all these skills have been tested when you passed the other CIMA exam papers.

- By the time you are in the exam room you will already have a clear idea of what does and doesn't make sense for this particular case. Unless the unseen material requires you to re-evaluate its position, the chances are that your first instinct is the right one. Make that your argument and stick to it.

What will come up in the exam?

In many respects, does it matter what you are required to do in the exam? If you have absorbed all the pre-seen material, you should be in good shape for dealing with the unseen material and the requirements of the paper.

Be ready for a 'twist' in the unseen. Make sure that when you prepare a report, you do what you are asked to. The number work is unlikely to be as demanding as in other CIMA exam papers, but you need to be prepared to do prepare some accurate calculations, and to explain in your report what they signify.

Be ready for anything.

If you have done your preparation properly, you might even be looking forward to learning about 'what happens next' in the unseen material.

Good luck with your exam!

D plc Pre-seen material and initial thoughts

Chapter learning objectives

This chapter contains the pre-seen information for the D plc house building case study, together with some initial thoughts on the usefulness of the information provided.

1 The industry: house-building

House-Building Industry Background

Modern methods of house-building have much in common with the manufacture of consumer durables like automobiles, washing machines, TVs and other like products. Indeed a small but increasing number of houses are manufactured using assembly line principles in a factory but there the similarity ends.

All houses have to be built on land and land for house-building is generally in short supply because it is designated for other uses be this for agriculture, industrial production, leisure, shopping centres, airports, roads, national parks and so on. It is also the case that in many countries the best land has already been built on, to form existing towns and cities.

Initial thoughts

- *You may believe that most building uses fairly traditional methods. However, there have been advances in the use of more environmentally friendly designs, processes and materials and a drive towards greater energy efficiency. Some firms are even using assembly line principles. Expect this to be an important trend that D plc will have to consider, either as an opportunity or as a threat (SWOT).*

- *Acquiring land at a good price in the right location is a CSF – this is covered in more detail in next section.*

Characteristics of House-Building

In most modern countries the state, via systems of local government, controls the use of land and this means that house-building firms and individuals have to seek planning permission to build on a particular piece of land and, depending on zoning regulations imposed by the state, may or may not be allowed to build. In some developing countries such regulation is not yet a reality.

A feature of house-building is its variety, both as regards building materials and styles. House styles also vary enormously and have been influenced by history and culture over the centuries ranging from the rows of linked town houses to the castle in the mountains. That said, the advent of global television coverage has led to some convergence in tastes and western-style houses can increasingly be found in the affluent suburbs of towns and cities throughout the world. In some countries houses are built primarily for rent by either private contractors or local government; in others, houses are built by private firms and sold at a profit to home buyers. In some countries there are combinations of these systems.

Another feature of house-building is that houses tend to be durable and can provide a home for different occupants over hundreds of years. A knock-on effect of this is that newly built houses have their market price determined to a considerable extent by the prevailing market price of the existing stock of houses.

A further characteristic is the enormous cost of houses in some countries. In many cases families need to take out a loan or mortgage to purchase their home and spend decades repaying the loan. The cost of house-building to individuals and society in general has been made clear most forcibly in recent years by the global financial crisis. In 2007 a significant number of house buyers who had borrowed in the years of high economic growth were unable to meet their mortgage payments and defaulted on their loans. This left the banks, which had made the loans, unable to meet their obligations and this contributed to a banking crisis which in turn left many Western governments with no alternative but to bail out some of their banks. For the housing market this is a particularly bad time because the banks, nervous about lending to house buyers with a poor credit record and or doubtful employment prospects, are reluctant to lend to these people and so demand for new houses tends to be confined to the financially better off.

Initial thoughts

- *As mentioned above, acquiring land at a good price in the right location is a CSF.*

- *Countries without firm planning regulations could present major opportunities but think about the ethical implications of, for example, demolishing ancient woodland to build houses and the impact on the firm's reputation.*

- *In countries with tighter planning laws gaining planning permission and having a good relationship with planning authorities could be a CSF. Could also be an opportunity for the examiner to present an issue relating to bribery and/or corruption in the unseen!*

- *More generally a governments attitude to planning and changes in legislation could be key PEST issues.*

- *The variation in house styles makes it difficult for firms to gain economies of scale through standardisation, especially across national boundaries. Convergence will make this easier and it is no surprise that overseas expansion is considered later in the case.*

- *The demand for new houses can be highly volatile, being linked to population growth, divorce rates, social changes, interest rates, state of the economy, etc. Many economies have seen boom and bust cycles in their housing markets.*

- *The current UK economic downturn is a major PEST issue and threat. However, there are still opportunities but builders need to be flexible in targeting growing market segments.*

House-building in the United Kingdom (UK)

The house-building company chosen for consideration in this case, (D plc House Builders) is located in the UK and so it is useful to outline some of the major features of the house-building industry in that country.

Initial thoughts

- *Interesting that we are given a specific country - the UK. This would emphasise the importance of researching real world companies to help understand the market in more detail.*

Structure of the Industry

The private house-building industry has been the major provider of new homes in the UK since the 1950's. House builders range from very large companies operating nationally to very small businesses serving individual local markets. During the late 1990s there was a decline in the number of small house- building firms but this reduction now seems to have stabilised. There is a good deal of movement in the market as firms enter and leave and a process of mergers and consolidations has taken place over time so that there are now a small number of large national companies that account for a significant number of house completions. Only a few UK house builders operate in overseas markets but the current economic climate in the home market has led a number of builders being willing to consider building outside the UK.

Most of the larger firms are publicly-quoted companies but further down the scale, private ownership is increasingly common. In the larger companies, 80% of shares tend to be held by institutional investors, pension fund holders and the like. Below the top ten (in terms of revenue earned per year), house builders are increasingly likely to concentrate their activities in specific regions, rather than operating nationwide. The top ten house builders now build about half of the total number of new houses. Large site developments account for an increasingly large share of new houses.

> *Initial thoughts*
>
> - *It is worth considering here what competitive advantage is gained by being a large company. These could include the following:*
>   - *Greater bargaining power when purchasing prime development sites.*
>   - *Dealing with major suppliers.*
>   - *Being able to win and deliver larger developments.*
>   - *Economies of scale (e.g. in marketing).*
>   - *Greater expertise in pursuing planning applications.*
> - *If you consider these to be significant, then a strategy of growth by acquisition could be advocated.*
> - *However, there is still room for smaller players, suggesting that the above advantages are not decisive, especially if firms have a local focus.*
> - *Similarly you could think about why overseas expansion is rare. The cost of transporting materials, the variation in planning regulations and processes and regional variations in taste all reduce the advantages of international firms over domestic rivals.*

Local Housing Markets

Although the largest house builders operate nationwide, there is very little housing demand that is really national. Housing demand and supply are local. These local markets have fuzzy boundaries, and many of them overlap. House buyers frequently decide on where to buy a house on the basis of the distance they are prepared to travel to work, or to reach schools or other local services. Which house they buy depends on the quality and price of their future home as well as its location. House prices vary significantly from very high prices in London to relatively low prices in some other parts of the UK.

Because the demand for houses exists locally it follows that house builders seek to ensure they are very well informed about what the local market demands. Most new houses are built without having a specific customer in mind but building firms rely on their own general understanding of the local market. Because of their acquired local knowledge, building firms are able to assess accurately how to obtain the best value from the development of a particular site. This specialised local information gives existing companies a competitive edge over less well informed new entrants.

Most local housing markets are dominated by sales of existing built homes. In business terms, this means that the price of new houses is largely determined by the prevailing price for existing houses. House builders therefore need to understand what the local housing market demands at the prevailing price levels.

Initial thoughts

- *This section develops the previous theme of competitive advantage and also brings in some Porter's 5 forces issues, such as the threat from new entrants.*

- *The fact that demand only exists locally again questions the extent to which national firms have an advantage over regional rivals. This section also highlights another CSF - the importance of understanding local tastes and demand.*

- *House prices are dependent on location - e.g. higher in London - and there is little that house builders can do to influence this. This means that land prices (driven by property prices) will also be something builders can do little about.*

Planning System

The most important constraint on housing supply at the present time is the shortage of land suitable for building. This is partly due to the current economic situation in which previously potential housing developments are no longer profitable. The underlying cause, however, is a continuing shortage of residential land being made available through the planning system.

This planning system requires all those who wish to make use of land to go through a planning application process in which applicants apply to regional, city, or other local government units for permission to make use of land for a particular purpose.

The problem of obtaining planning permission adds significantly to the cost of house-building in the UK. The duty of ensuring that the country's planning policies are enforced falls to local government which typically maintains a planning division or department made up of professional planners whose task it is to scrutinise planning applications and then recommend to the local government's elected council whether or not the plans submitted by house builders should be given approval. Most applications for minor matters are dealt with by the planning professionals under a system of delegated authority but are subject to confirmation by the council. Sometimes, to the great frustration of house-building companies, plans which actually meet the criteria laid down in national planning legislation are refused by the local government authority on political grounds because of objections by local people. An appeals procedure for refused applications does exist but where appeals are lodged this adds to delays and causes additional costs for the house builders concerned.

It is also through the planning system that central and local government seeks to achieve balanced development in the sense of ensuring that whenever house-building on any scale takes place, the needs of the new house dwellers and local community will be catered for in terms of a wide range of social, educational, recreational, health and other provisions. In particular local government is charged by central government to ensure that space is provided for shopping centres, playing fields, medical centres and so on.

In November 2011 the UK Government passed the Localism Act which gave more powers to local communities to influence planning decisions in their locality and to simplify and reform the planning systems in order to create a presumption in favour of sustainable development. Another justification for this change was to improve the efficiency of the planning system and to make more land available for businesses and for housing development in a time of severe economic difficulty. This legislation produced a negative reaction from a range of interest groups concerned with the protection of the countryside but house-building firms generally welcomed the planning reforms.

A constraint on house builders in the UK is the policy of successive governments to require house builders to re-use 'brownfield land' for house-building purposes so as to avoid swallowing up yet more 'greenfield land'.

Note: 'Brownfield land' is land that is or was formerly occupied by a permanent building that has become derelict or vacant and now has the potential for redevelopment. By contrast, most of the land in the UK is 'greenfield'. 'Greenfield land' is simply land that has not been developed before.

For house builders this policy presents a problem because brownfield land is generally more costly to prepare for building development. It often involves the costly process of ensuring vacant possession of existing buildings, the demolition of any such buildings and the remediation of land by clearing it of any toxic substances that might have been left by previous industrial users and so on. The state via the local authorities has often provided a subsidy to help in the preparation of brownfield land for housing development and the UK Government plans to encourage building firms and local authorities to form partnerships for joint development of brownfield sites.

Note: It is important to distinguish greenfield land from the 'green belt'. Preserving the green belt is a policy used for controlling urban growth. The idea is for a ring of countryside where urbanisation will be resisted for the foreseeable future. The fundamental aim of green belt policy is to prevent urban sprawl by keeping land permanently open. The disadvantage of this policy for house builders is that it is very difficult to obtain planning permission to build in areas designated as green belt.

Initial thoughts

- *The shortage of suitable land in the UK will always result in high competition and high prices in popular areas. (Note: this is not necessarily a negative if the end result is higher house prices - the key issue is **margins**).*

- *This would also support a policy of developing a land bank and buying suitable land when it becomes available, even if there are not plans to build on it yet.*

- *The information on the planning process reinforces earlier thoughts on the importance of having (local) expertise in this area. Furthermore larger firms may have more power to lobby government and afford appeals.*

- *Key PEST issues:*
  - *government changes to planning laws (e.g. Localism Act),*
  - *availability of greenbelt v greenfield v brownfield sites,*
  - *emphasis on mix of properties built (including social housing),*
  - *incentives to develop brownfield sites,*
  - *potential for protests against site developments on conservation grounds.*

- *Some brownfield sites may require specialist knowledge to ensure toxic chemicals are disposed off correctly to make the site clean.*

Other Constraints

A further perceived constraint is the high and growing regulatory burden. This includes a range of issues, from planning requirements through to building regulations, health and safety legislation and sustainability policies.

Sustainability policies have been developed in response to fear of exhaustion of natural resources and of the probable impact of climate change. Indeed, climate change has established itself as a major issue which requires an urgent and coordinated global response. One consequence of global warming is an increase in extreme weather conditions. In recent decades the south-east of the UK has experienced a decline in its annual rainfall with the result that in some years drought conditions have prevailed. By contrast some other parts of the UK have suffered extensive flooding in the autumn and winter months.

Both these problems have led to calls by environmentalists for building to be restricted in low lying areas subject to flood and in those parts of the south-east that have suffered drought conditions. To help tackle global warming, the UK Government announced in October 2008 an ambitious target committing the UK to cut greenhouse gas emissions by 80% by the middle of this century. This commitment required carbon reductions to be made by all industries including the housing sector. The UK Government highlighted the house-building industry as a key sector where carbon reductions could be made and the Government has consequently announced a zero carbon target to be achieved by 2016 for all newly built houses.

The recent economic situation has compounded the problems of the industry making it difficult for house builders to borrow money and for would-be house purchasers to raise mortgage finance.

Finally, there is widespread concern in the UK about the recent contraction of the industry and the reduction in supply chain capacity that has occurred as a result of the economic downturn.

Initial thoughts

- *Climate change will impact local needs in terms of housing - e.g. location, flood protection.*
- *Sustainability is a major issue in this case:*
  - *cutting greenhouse gases*
  - *zero carbon target for all new houses by 2016*
  - *This will impact energy efficiency, choice of building materials, etc*
- *Current credit crunch again emphasised with the implication that the UK market is unlikely to see rapid growth for some time (another PEST issue).*

Land Banks

In order to ensure that they always have a ready supply of land on which to build, house builders in the UK build up 'land banks'. These land banks contain two main types of land, 'strategic land' and 'short term land'. Strategic land is land without formal planning permission but which a building firm anticipates might be allowed planning permission in the future, and short term land is land that has planning permission in principle already granted, but which requires more detailed planning permission before an actual house-building development is allowed to take place on it.

The processes of acquisition, applying for planning permission and preparation of land on which to build houses consume a great deal of a house builder's limited resources. House builders seek to build up a stock of strategic land which they aim to convert to short term land complete with planning permission granted for current house-building use. Large house builders commonly have stocks of land which will provide them with a supply sufficient to meet anticipated demand for 5 or 6 years ahead. Smaller builders will have smaller land banks because potential building land is very costly and ties up capital in the business that cannot immediately be converted into revenue to build houses.

One of the problems for house builders in the land bank acquisition process is that the more likely that land is to receive planning permission, the more expensive it becomes to purchase, as rival house builders compete to obtain the best land. Another problem for house builders is how quickly they should use their land bank stock to build houses. They are under pressure from investors to use the land as quickly as possible to generate profits and dividends. However, they need to ration out the use of their land bank to ensure that they have a sufficient supply of land to build houses to meet current demand and so satisfy investors' expectations year-on-year into the future.

Initial thoughts

- *It is worth considering the relative pros and cons of the two approaches mentioned.*

- *Strategic land:*
  - *Pros - cheaper so ultimately better margins, less pressure to buy land at short notice if deemed to be overpriced.*

  - *Cons - higher risk that planning permission will not be gained, need for large sums of capital tied up, pressure from shareholders to use up or sell sooner than ideal.*

- *Short-term land:*
  - *Pros - lower risk that planning permission will not be gained, less capital tied up.*

  - *Cons - land will be more expensive so ultimately lower margins, more pressure to buy land at short notice to meet demand.*

Standardisation of House-Building

House builders have improved the efficiency of house-building over the years. Perhaps the greatest improvements in efficiency have come from the standardisation process. By virtue of trial and error and learning from fellow builders they have hit upon a house design that can have a variety of standardised elevations and features but allows the builder on large sites to build with less cost and in less time than when houses are tailor-made for individuals.

Standardisation has many advantages including the use of standard drawings and specifications that reduce the design costs as compared with customised buildings. This helps facilitate the efficient sequencing of trades and allows subcontractors to make use of relatively low cost semi-skilled labour as in the classic scientific management approach; materials can also be purchased in bulk on long term supply contracts at a discount and standardising the internal design of buildings makes it possible to obtain the maximum cost effective use of space in the minimum area.

Differentiation is achieved by the selective use of standardised features which are often just attached to standard design houses such as porticos, black and white wall planks and bay windows.

Initial thoughts

- *It is interesting to consider whether standardisation could be a source of competitive advantage. You could argue that it is a **threshold** competence - i.e. builders have to be able to do this simply to be competitive but does not convey an advantage. On the other hand it might enable larger firms to gain economies of scale and further cost savings because they have more scope to roll out the standard house.*

- *The aspects described as contributing to differentiation all appear to be easy to replicate so would not form the basis of a sustainable competitive advantage. This could emphasise the importance of reputation/brand, expertise in building more energy efficient houses and so on.*

- *Another angle could be to suggest that some firms may be able to operate in a niche by building houses that look nothing like the standard mass produced new builds of the big firms.*

Subcontracting

A limited but increasing amount of pre-fabrication occurs but the bulk of construction from the foundation levels upward is carried out on site by subcontracted bricklayers, joiners, roofers, plasterers, plumbers, electricians, glaziers, painters and so on and each major stage is inspected by local authority building control officers to ensure that the construction is in line with agreed plans and meets basic quality and health and safety standards.

The common system of labour subcontracting in the UK has some advantages; it enables a large national building contractor to hire local tradesmen near to the site where building is to take place and saves the cost of maintaining a large labour force and transporting it around the country. The draw-back to the system is the uneven quality of the labour employed and quality on site has to be closely monitored and enforced by a site manager or foreman.

> *Initial thoughts*
>
> - *This section again suggests that larger firms are not necessarily going to have cost or quality advantages over local rivals when it comes to labour costs. Infact both firms could be using the same sub-contractors and getting the work assessed by the same building control officers. However, the training and skills of site foremen could make a difference to the ultimate quality.*
>
> - *It is worth considering the pros and cons of subcontracting:*
>   - *Pros - only use when needed, lower fixed costs (and hence operating gearing), can benefit from their expertise, flexibility to switch suppliers if required.*
>   - *Cons - may be more expensive, quality control is more difficult, don't develop in-house core competences.*

Modern Methods of Construction (MMC)

MMC involves the manufacture of house parts offsite in a specially designed factory. The two main products are panels and modules.

Panels include ready-made walls, floors and roofs. These are transported to the site and assembled quickly, often within a day. Some panels have wiring and plumbing already inside them, making construction even faster.

Modules are ready-made rooms, which can be pieced together to make a whole house or flat but are used most frequently for bathrooms or kitchens. All the fittings are added in the factory. These modules are also known as 'pods'.

MMC can also include innovative site-based methods, such as use of concrete moulds. A range of materials is used for MMC, the most common being wood, steel and concrete, although many houses built in the UK using MMC have a brick outer layer and so look like traditional houses.

The latest 'Green Home' developments designed to comply with the UK Government's zero carbon agenda make use of most of the MMC materials and techniques and one of the UK's top building companies has already completed prototype zero carbon houses.

Those who state their support for MMC houses claim they have fewer defects, can be built more quickly, are more energy efficient, involve less transportation of materials, produce less waste, involve fewer accidents and have less impact on local residents during construction.

Those less keen on MMC claim that they involve higher immediate costs, poor public acceptability, and inflexibility of factories in responding to fluctuating demand.

> *Initial thoughts*
>
> - *This suggests that a firm without knowledge of MMC is at a disadvantage. However, it is worth considering the relative pros and cons of their use:*
> - *Advantages:*
>   - *Greater consistency of quality, fewer defects.*
>   - *Ability to build a new house much more quickly.*
>   - *Typically such firms give customers more choice in designing their own homes.*
>   - *May make it much easier to comply with 'Green home' and zero carbon targets.*
>   - *More environmentally friendly / sustainable in other areas as well - e.g. less transportation of materials, less waste, less impact on local community.*
>   - *Fewer accidents during the build.*
>   - *May be a source of differentiation compared to traditional build.*
> - *Disadvantages:*
>   - *higher immediate costs.*
>   - *poor public acceptability (note: such approaches are well known in countries such as Germany but rarer within the UK).*
>   - *Inflexibility of factories in responding to changes in demand. Difficult to assess how big an issue this is because once the elements have been constructed, the final assembly of the house can happen very quickly.*

Business Models

The business model adopted by most UK companies is known as the 'current trader model' (also known as the 'classical house builder model') which consists in essence of a cycle of land acquisition, development and outright sale. Profit is the margin between sale price and acquisition and development costs; the developer retains no long-term interest in the property.

Other models exist such as the 'investor model' in which the builder retains a long term interest in the developed site such as housing for rent or the retained portion of shared ownership sales; the self build model in which the individual owner contracts with others to do the building for him to his own specification and the RSL (Registered Social Landlord) build for sale model in which the RSL builds houses for sale as well as for rent. These other models have relatively few users to date.

Initial thoughts

- *It is worth researching the different models in more detail as the unseen may suggest a need for flexibility and /or a switch in approaches.*

- *Key issues when considering which approach to adopt include the following:*

  - ***Skills / competences** - being a landlord, acquiring and managing tenants require different skills to simply building and selling houses.*

  - ***Timescales** - would shareholders prefer the classical approach where the builder can move onto the next project once a build is finished and properties sold rather than the ongoing commitment needed under the investor model.*

  - ***Risk** - the investor model has the risk of failing to get sufficient tenants at a rent high enough to give a decent return.*

  - ***Return** - would the builder expect (and get!) a higher return from rentals rather than through sale? You could argue that if other investors can make money through buy-to-let schemes then why shouldn't the builder do the same? On the other hand, you could argue that the price of the property will reflect the present value of future rentals.*

  - ***Cash flow** - the investor model requires greater cash reserves than the classical approach. With the latter funds are recovered when the property is sold rather than seeing years of income with the investor model.*

2 The company: D House Builders plc

History

D House Builders plc, (referred to hereafter as D plc), one of the UK's top ten house builders, was originally established by Don Roby in 1969. D plc was first quoted on the London Stock Exchange in 1982. The Group's head office is based in the Company's Central Region.

In January 2001, the Company completed the acquisition of H plc, another listed UK house builder. Previous major acquisitions include the S Group in July 1981 and the R group of companies in April 1994.

D plc has steadily grown to become a nationwide house builder with operating businesses spread across the length and breadth of the UK. The Group trades under the brand names H, R and S.

The D plc house-building operation is the core business of the Group and builds houses using traditional designs comparable with its major competitors in almost all aspects of quality and service but does lag behind in its use of MMC. The wide range of property types includes three, four and five-bedroom detached properties, two and three-bedroom town houses and semi-detached houses, bungalows and apartments for the domestic market.

Initial thoughts

- *D plc is one of the major players in the UK industry, so it is worth looking back at previous comments on how/whether larger firms can gain a competitive advantage. While it offers a wide range of property types, it seems that D plc is not a differentiator but appears to be a very traditional building company and lags behind in the use of MMC.*

- *D plc is quoted meaning that it should find raising finance easier but will face more short -termist shareholder pressure and is likely to be subject to greater scrutiny, especially over its green and sustainability credentials.*

- *D plc has a history of acquisition as well as organic growth.*

- *The claimed advantages for this are*
  - *greater speed of growth,*
  - *results in fewer competitors,*
  - *gain expertise , transfer of skills and other synergy,*
  - *can be a way of getting around barriers to entry.*

- *The usual problems of acquisition are*
  - *paying too much for companies,*
  - *clash of cultures and other integration problems, resulting in*
  - *a failure to generate synergy.*

- *As you continue to find out more about D plc, look to see if there is any evidence of the benefits and synergies being gained or whether the typical problems are more evident.*

Brands

The H business provides a range of premium homes, in both modern and traditional styles. H has a solid reputation for the design and quality of the homes it builds. The R business builds good quality affordable homes for a wide range of customers and is concerned with the revival of local communities and the regeneration of older neighbourhoods.The S business focuses on low cost housing; this part of the business aims to get young buyers onto the housing ladder (i.e. into the property market).

- *By having three brands D plc can target specific market segments more effectively - e.g. H's image is not undermined by being associated with social housing. However, it does mean that some marketing economies will be lost.*

- *There is also the concern that different skills are needed for high quality and low cost housing with the risk that both are compromised.*

Board of Directors

There are nine members on D plc's Board of Directors. They include the Chairman, Chief Executive, three executive directors and four non-executive directors (NEDs). The executive directors have extensive experience in the house-building industry and provide a direct line of control between the Company and its operating businesses. The NEDs provide a balance to the Board and bring a wide breadth of experience and skills to its working.

The Board routinely meets seven times a year and has a formal annual schedule of matters reserved for its consideration and decision. This agreed schedule includes the approval of the Group's strategy, major investments, annual and half yearly results, interim management statements and trading updates, review of performance, dividend policy, risk monitoring and ensuring that adequate financial resources are available. The schedule is reviewed on an annual basis.

Initial thoughts

- *The make up of the board does seem to comply with governance best practice - roles of Chairman and CEO, presence of NEDs. However, we would need more detail on the existence or otherwise of remuneration committees, audit committees and so on, to make a more definitive statement here.*

- *On a positive note, the scope of the "schedule of matters" looks very comprehensive but the following concerns should also be noted:*

  - *everything sounds very formal,*

  - *the board only meet 7 times a year - once a month would be more typical,*

  - *the formal schedule is reviewed annually,*

  - *taken together these might suggest a lack of flexibility and an inability to discuss and respond to changing market conditions or, at worse, a crisis.*

Organisation and Management Structure

The organisational structure of D plc has evolved largely as a result of a series of mergers and acquisitions over the years since its formation. The Company started in what is now the Company's Central Region, grew organically in the early years but since then has expanded by a series of mergers and acquisitions into a national company with three regional divisions: Central, Northern and Eastern.

When businesses were acquired in other parts of the country they were allowed to operate with a degree of autonomy. This was often a matter of convenience as senior management lacked the commitment to rationalise the differing practices and systems of the newly acquired and existing businesses into a coherent centralised system.

When five years ago the present regional divisional structure of Central, Northern and Eastern was formalised, an attempt was made to ensure that common systems and ways of working were adopted across each of the three regions but again, because of the pressures on the Company at the time, was never carried through as intended.

One outcome of this is that each regional division uses some working practices and systems inherited from when H, R and S were acquired. One of the most evident of these is the existence of different IT systems in each of the three regional divisions. This has limited impact within the regions themselves but makes for some difficulties when coordinated action is required across the Company.

Another problem created by the semi-autonomous regional divisional structure arises when close cooperation is required as on joint-projects at the boundary of each division. The degree of autonomy allowed to regional divisional managers often results in rivalry and conflict over how things should be managed between them.

Initial thoughts

- *The potential pitfalls of growth by acquisition were mentioned earlier. Unfortunately it appears that some of these problems have materialised for D plc:*
  - *failure to integrate business units - e.g. lack of standardisation of IT systems,*
  - *lack of central control results in rivalry and conflict between divisions.*
- *(Note: it is not totally clear whether each region has its own separate IT system or whether each H unit has kept the IT from the acquisition of H or...?)*
- *This will result in a failure to generate synergies.*
- *It is also worrying that senior management have lacked the commitment to make necessary changes in the past. This could indicate that there might be problems implementing suggested future changes.*

A diagram of the Organisational Structure can be found in **Appendix 1**.

Management Structure

The Group is ultimately governed by its Board of Directors. Each of the three regional divisions is controlled by a Divisional Board, headed by a General Manager. Each Division has 3 regional operating businesses, (trading as the original 3 companies H, R and S). These 3 companies are headed within each region by a managing director and a management team with local knowledge and experience. The executive management teams each have wide experience.

Corporate Governance.

D plc's Board acknowledges that by adopting and implementing the highest standards of corporate governance that this sets the standards and values for the entire Company. The Company seeks to comply with best practice in all areas of corporate governance and continues to review the Company's procedures to maintain proper control and accountability. D plc also claims to seek integration of sustainability policies and procedures into its normal business activities to ensure that when building new houses it takes into account the impact on the environment. Like most of the larger house builders, D plc is developing detailed policies to cover all contingencies.

Initial thoughts

- *This all seems very commendable but we have very little real detail or evidence to assess, unlike some previous cases.*

The House-Building Process in D plc

The process of house-building adopted by D plc conforms to what is known in the industry as the 'classical house builder' model. Firms using this model acquire land, seek planning permission and undertake all the development and build tasks such as initial evaluation of the project, land preparation, construction of the houses or apartments and marketing and sales through to the final house-purchaser.

Many of the houses built by D plc are built ahead of contracts for sale with planning forecasts based on recent sales data. This has sometimes been referred to as 'speculative building' but D plc, like many UK firms, has long experience in the business and knows its local markets extremely well.

D plc, through its regional operating businesses H, R and S, manages construction work itself and directly purchases most of the materials but it contracts out much actual building work to sub-contractors. Specialist tasks such as initial design will also often be carried out by independent agencies, working to contract. Standard house designs are generally built although the actual designs will vary from site to site.

D plc has a core staff in its regional operating companies that decides on and controls all the activities required for building but it contracts out development functions to planning specialists and architects. D plc sometimes uses specialist sub-contractors to undertake on-site building tasks under the control of the firm's own site managers and senior management teams.

Initial thoughts

- *It is difficult to see what in-house expertise and competences D plc has as much of the process (e.g. design, construction) is contracted out. This again raises the issue of how and whether D plc has a sustainable competitive advantage.*

- *Speculative building may carry higher risk, again stressing the importance of local knowledge.*

The Strategy of D plc

D plc's primary objective is to remain one of the leading national house builders, building homes ranging from low-cost starter homes to large premium family homes. Its strategy to achieve this objective is to build on existing skills and competences, while maintaining firm cost control and continuing to produce quality homes that customers want to buy.

Initial thoughts

- *This section really doesn't say very much!*

- *As stated previously, it is not obvious what the "existing skills and competences" comprise. Only two aspects are specified here - cost control and understanding what customers want. Look to discuss these further.*

Company Performance

The Board considered that D plc delivered a good performance for the year ended 31 December 2011 despite challenging conditions. The results for 2011 reflect the implementation of a strategy of firm cost control, maximisation of sales revenues and pursuit of strong cash generation. During 2011 D plc increased the number of housing units it completed. D plc therefore increased its revenue, margins and profit as compared with 2010. However, the Company decided not to declare a dividend given the present economic climate.

The Company's record over the last five years along with accompanying financial information and notes from the Finance Director can be found in Appendix 2.

> *Initial thoughts (Note: please look at appendix 2 when considering this section)*
>
> * *On the face of it, D plc has done very well to improve performance over 2010. Furthermore, we are told that the causes behind the improvement are better cost control, maximisation of sales revenues and strong cash generation.*
>
> * *More detailed analysis is required to assess this view in more depth and to assess performance to date. This is done in chapter 3.*
>
> * *The lack of dividend could be a concern to some shareholders.*

Operations and Constraints

As a very traditional company, D plc has stayed clear of the use of MMC preferring instead to retain the tried and tested house-building methods. That said, the current recession together with UK Government pressure to reduce carbon emissions has encouraged some of D plc's competitors to adopt some modern methods of construction and in this respect D plc is in danger of being left behind.

D plc has threshold competences in most areas of its value chain activities and enjoys distinctive core competences in its knowledge of local markets. There are, however, reasons for concern in that some of its activities will need to be addressed if D plc is to remain a major player in the premier league of house- building.

The Company has always had a good working relationship with its bankers and financial institutions. It is therefore anticipated that funding will be available for future projects where these are justified.

In the boom years, the business performed well but since the UK housing market went into decline following the sub-prime crisis of 2007, D plc's business has not performed as well as its key competitors. The existing board members have been in place for many years and the Chairman and Chief Executive have not seen any reason to change the way D plc does its business. From the perspective of most members of the board, the current downturn is just part of another business cycle and the strategy employed by D plc has been to continue with business as usual until the worst is over.

NN, one of the NEDs is of a different opinion. She thinks that sticking to the existing way of doing things is a recipe for disaster. She argues that the recent performance of the industry leader, increasing competition by new entrants from continental Europe, the UK Government's zero carbon agenda and the threat posed by the effects of climate change in the south-east of the UK, all require a much more proactive response by D plc. She also feels that in many areas of the business, such as the application of IT, the adoption of MMC, the training of staff, and the sourcing of supplies, D plc is falling behind the best in the business. In brief its operational methods need urgent attention if the Company is to emerge from the recession to compete effectively. Given that the last review of the Company's strategic position was before the collapse of the housing market, she feels that another review is now essential.

Initial thoughts (Note: please look at appendix 2 when considering this section)

- *Again the link is made between MMC and meeting government targets for carbon emissions. D plc must look at this area more seriously to avoid being left behind.*

- *Remember that threshold competences merely allow one to meet customers' minimum requirements and therefore to continue to exist. They do not convey competitive advantage.*

- *It is suggested that D plc has core competences in "its knowledge of local markets". Core competences are activities that underpin competitive advantage and are difficult for competitors to imitate or obtain. You could discuss how difficult it is to obtain such local knowledge and hence the risk of D plc's advantage being eroded by local rivals.*

- *It is anticipated that funding will be available for future projects but again it may be wise to be sceptical, given the ongoing credit crunch and recession*

- *The most worrying part of this section is the comment that D plc has not performed as well as its key competitors following the sub-prime crisis of 2007. This problem is made worse by the reluctance of the entrenched board to believe they have a problem to address.*

- *The comments from NN identifies some useful **threats** to consider putting on your SWOT:*
  - *performance of the industry leader, although we are not told what this might be,*
  - *increasing competition from new entrants from continental Europe. (This might suggest that a strong brand name does not form an effective barrier to entry and may not be worth as much as we would like to think.)*
  - *the UK government's zero-carbon agenda,*
  - *climate change in the SE of England.*

- *She has also identified possible **weaknesses***
  - *application of IT,*
  - *adoption of MMC,*
  - *staff training (the first time this has been mentioned),*
  - *sourcing of supplies (again this is the first indication of a possible problem in this area).*

- *Note that these are just NN's opinions - you will need to consider evidence for or against these views.*

- *The last sentence will be seen by many as a hot exam tip - you will be asked to do the strategic review mentioned. A SWOT analysis features in most cases but is rarely an explicit requirement and there is no guarantee it will be this time. However, ensure you can formulate a SWOT, appraise and prioritise its points and have some ideas as to what the company could do about it. These themes are discussed in more detail in chapter 4.*

- *Finally it is again worrying that the last strategic review was before the collapse of the housing market, again indicating a complete lack of flexibility and responsiveness to market conditions.*

Overseas Investment

D plc's Board is well aware that some of its competitors have overseas operations but D plc has been put off seeking expansion abroad to date because of the risks involved. It is also aware that some of the UK's bigger house builders have pulled out of the US market following its dramatic decline in the last few years. It also appreciates the large amount of preliminary work involved in any thorough assessment of an overseas market and the analysis of the competition and changing business environment that needs to be carried out before opportunities and threats in any overseas market can be ascertained.

Despite these reservations, the current and likely future economic situation and other problems associated with house-building in the UK is making some Board members think again. According to the International Monetary Fund (IMF), the global economy is now in what it calls a 'two speed recovery process'. Advanced economies are either growing slowly or are stagnating, with unsustainable debt levels and persistently high unemployment. Developing economies, on the other hand, are experiencing strong growth, as they continue to invest in their own infrastructure, grow overall exports, and start to see increased levels of consumption from their own countries' residents. It is within the context of these changing global conditions that some members of D plc's Board have shifted from their long standing reluctance to seriously consider the possibility of expansion overseas.

Initial thoughts

- *D plc has not sought overseas expansion to date due to the risks involved. It is worth considering what those risks might be:*
  - *the need to understand local market conditions - especially the risk of making houses that customers don't want to buy,*
  - *if the overseas venture is quite small then D plc would not be able to get any bulk discounts on buying materials and it would be too expensive to transport from the UK,*
  - *the risk of failing to fully understand local planning regulations and processes,*
  - *wider political risk due to political instability, terrorism or even war,*
  - *the risk of economic downturns in that country,*
  - *forex risk,*
  - *the reaction of local rivals.*
- *It is for the above reasons that preliminary research is vital.*
- *The IMF report, however, indicates that strong growth may be possible in some countries, despite market conditions in the UK. This is why D plc is considering such a strategy.*

The Building Industry in Country Y

D plc's Board has considered moving into Country Y in Asia. There are a number of reasons for this. First the Sales Director of D plc already has some familiarity with and contacts in the house-building industry in the Country by virtue of frequent visits to family and friends. Indeed by a stroke of good fortune one of his relatives happens to own a small building company in that Country.

Secondly, the development of the building industry in Country Y has necessarily been quite rapid in recent decades as the economy has moved from that founded on an agricultural base to one based increasingly on manufacturing and services. Like many other countries in Asia the process of industrialisation has been accompanied by one of urbanisation as people have moved to better-paid employment in towns and cities which have grown in size. This migration from the countryside to the towns has created a massive demand for housing and building firms have taken advantage of the opportunities presented to grow and expand their operations. The outcome has been the development of a dynamic building industry with a mix of firms of all sizes.

The last decade in particular has been one of rapid economic progress and Country Y's economy has grown by about 7% per annum over the period. This has produced a growing middle class with an income level that allows citizens to enjoy a life-style only dreamt of by their parents. One of the most evident signs of this life-style is that families can now have a family home that provides spacious accommodation with all the facilities that have come to be expected in a modern society. Housing styles vary considerably from apartments within large housing developments to detached, semi-detached and terraced housing that is increasingly being built in the suburbs of the towns and cities of the Country. Over time the traditional timber homes that once constituted the bulk of housing in Country Y have been replaced by housing built of the more durable materials of concrete, steel, brick and tiles. Many of these new houses and apartments are modelled on western-style buildings that derive from the presence of European and American people during the past colonial era. In Country Y the influence of UK housing styles on its own housing styles is particularly evident, especially in the growing suburbs where detached and semi-detached houses of brick construction have become the preferred choice of many increasingly affluent families.

It is this demand for traditional brick built houses that has caught the attention of the Sales Director of D plc. On his regular visits to family and friends in Country Y, he has become aware of both the demand for UK style brick housing and of the demand for skills and expertise in this type of house-building.

Whilst opportunities exist, overseas investment always carries an element of risk and the Sales Director is very much aware that the political stability of the country is of recent origin and that the multi-ethnic mix of the population has been the source of armed conflict in the past and that this has toppled some previous governments in Country Y. Some of these groups contain militant members who still harbour a simmering resentment for the injustices they see as perpetrated by the government. There is therefore a risk that this feature of Country Y has the potential to upset the stability and working of its Government.

The Sales Director is also mindful of some of the differences that exist between Country Y and the UK in the area of corporate governance and social responsibility requirements and in the potential for difficulties for any UK company considering a merger or joint-venture with a building company in Country Y. A feature of business in some Asian countries is that control of companies by large family groups is common. One of the features of this ownership structure is that it provides power to insiders to pursue their own interests at the expense of minority shareholders, creditors and other stakeholders. Though Country Y has adequate corporate governance codes in place, the weak rule of law and the existence of possible corruption at different levels within the country make it difficult to ensure enforcement of governance principles.

There are also some additional specific concerns confronting the building industry in Country Y that have little parallel in the UK. The first of these has to do with the fact that Country Y is located in an area that is subject to relatively frequent earthquake activity. Country Y is also in a typhoon belt which seasonally produces very strong winds so that builders have to allow for these natural hazards when considering house design.

Initial thoughts

- *Advantages of investing in Y include the following:*
  - *rapid growth,*
  - *increasing demand for UK-style housing and the skills and expertise needed to build them.*

- *Disadvantages and potential problems include the following:*
  - *the need to acquire the CSF of local knowledge,*
  - *political instability, including militant groups with "simmering resentment",*
  - *risk of earthquakes and typhoons will influence designs. This is not an area of expertise D plc currently has,*
  - *differences in governance and social responsibility will either mean D plc has higher costs than local rivals (if it maintains current high standards) or exposes it to reputational risk back in the UK if it adopts local standards,*
  - *similarly local corruption could make it difficult for D plc to compete without adopting similar practices,*
  - *expansion via merger of joint venture would be difficult. This could be a real problem as some form of joint arrangement would normally be the optimal approach here to gain local expertise and knowledge,*
  - *family strength and control would be an issue if D plc worked with a local firm as the family may be used to pursuing "their own interests" at D plc's expense.*

- *Given the Sales Director's contacts in country Y, there is definitely scope for dubious business practices, especially if the Sales Director is involved in making any decisions regarding the venture. To what extent are his views designed to maximise D plc's shareholder wealth or are they to benefit friends, family and himself?*

3 Appendix 1

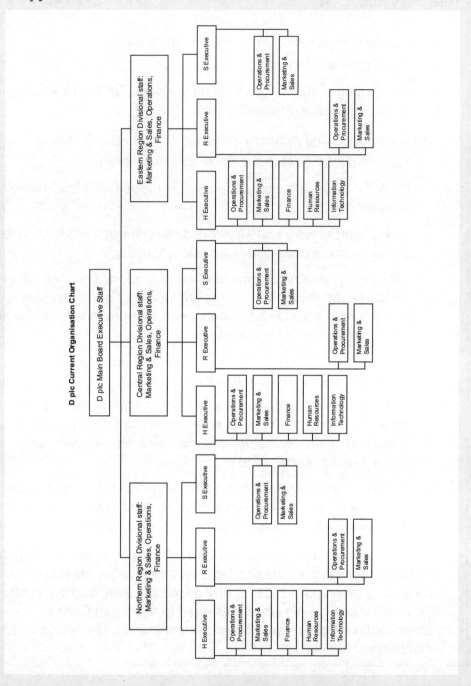

Notes to Organisation Chart

D plc operates with the main board responsible for overall strategic and policy decisions of the group. These are then enacted through the regional structure and it is in turn the responsibility of the appropriate company to market, build and sell individual properties.

The separate companies within the group are responsible for carrying out these activities via their various departmental and administrative systems. All three companies H, R and S within each region have marketing, sales, operations and procurement functions. Some rationalisation and cost savings have recently been achieved with company H in each region also taking on responsibility for the finance, human resources and information technology functions for all companies within their region.

Initial thoughts

- *Some comments on the divisional structure were made under the heading "Organisation and Management Structure" above.*

- *The move for H to take on all regional finance, HR and IT is an interesting idea. On the one hand it should result in cost savings and for HR and finance there is unlikely to be much difference between the H, R and S. However, for IT, there could be big differences between the systems operated (although this is unclear from the material provided).*

---

4 Appendix 2

Finance Director's Internal Report to accompany D plc's results for 2011

(Prepared prior to the Annual General Meeting in April 2012)

The market continues to improve slightly but domestic credit restrictions for first time buyers and lack of confidence in the buy-to-let market means that this remains a challenging environment for the business. Against this background, financial performance improved significantly in 2011 with property completions of 9673 (2010: 9582) generating sales value of £1,644.4 million (2010: £1,533.1 million) and operating profit at £131.6 million (2010: £53.7 million).

This was as a result of an improved mix of sales resulting in an increased average selling price of £170,000 per completion. Regional details as follows:

Region	Average selling price £	% Total property completions sold
Eastern	250,000	20
Central	153,000	60
Northern	141,000	20

Whilst there now appears to be some stability in the market this is not anticipated to result in any increase in completion volumes, and for forecasting purposes it is predicted that completions will be 9500 per year for the next 3 years, split in the same proportions per region, at an average sales value of £170,000 each.

Additions to and usage of the land bank are expected to be broadly neutral over the next 3 years, additions being funded from operational cash flows. It is unlikely, that the sales volumes seen in 2007-2009 will be achievable for the foreseeable future, unless consideration is given to operating outside traditional markets and if this is considered the rapid expansion of housing demand in some developing countries may warrant investigation.

To build on and improve the operating performance for the foreseeable future it will be necessary for the Company to maximise the value achieved for each completion through build cost reduction and revised planning developments in order to optimise resources. It is anticipated that operational changes proposed and the results of a procurement review are anticipated to save just under 10% on direct costs from 2012 onwards, and have been incorporated in the forecast results attached, with forecast gross margin of 22.0%, a considerable improvement on previous years (2011:13.6%, 2010:10%). Forecast profit and cash flows, assuming a successful cost reduction programme are attached.

An overhead cost reduction exercise has resulted in operating expenses being reduced by £8.1 million, just over 8 % between 2010 and 2011, the savings coming from optimising administrative resources and improvements in IT systems. It is unlikely that any further reduction can be achieved and in fact for forecasting purposes it is assumed that there will be just over a 3% year-on-year increase in operating expenses. Further savings may be achievable if a major review of the current IT systems is undertaken, but this will inevitably involve capital investment.

Finance costs have reduced with the repayment of loans and borrowings, and whilst this is a stable situation for the short term, the longer term funding of the business will require careful consideration. A £250 million loan note is repayable in 2015. It is anticipated that the funding cost of the business with an average interest cost of 8% will remain at the current level over the next 3 years.

For forecasting purposes it is assumed that finance costs will remain constant at £31.9 million over the forecast period (2012-2014)

Cash flow is expected to remain positive in line with the steady state of predicted sales completions and planned cost reductions. No major fixed asset purchases or sales are planned. No significant movements in working capital are expected over the forecast period.

The corporation tax rate is assumed to remain at 28%.

Initial thoughts (Note: more detailed financial analysis of the exhibits in appendix 2 will be carried out in Chapter 3. However, based on the FD's report we can make the following preliminary comments)

- *Given the ongoing recession, the FD is correct in stating that D plc's improved performance is impressive, although elsewhere it has been indicated that rivals have performed better.*

- *Sales*
  - *Sales up by 7.26% but completions by 0.95%.*
  - *The main reason for higher sales is the fact that the average selling price is up 6.25% from £160,000 to £170,000. This is due to a change in sales mix towards more expensive properties, especially in the Eastern region.*
  - *We are told that completion volumes are unlikely to grow over the next 3 years.*
  - *Furthermore, no future change in mix is anticipated meaning that unless property prices grow generally, there is no increase in sales revenue expected.*

- *Profit and margins*
  - *Operating profit has increased by 145% and operating margins have increased from 3.5% to 8.0% due to an 8% cut in operating expenses.*
  - *Going forwards there is little scope for further cuts to operating costs so D plc is looking at cutting direct costs to boost profits*

- *Evaluation of cost cutting strategy*
  - *Cutting operating expenses has clearly been successful in boosting profits. However, we are not given any detail here, other than the fact (earlier) that company H in each region has taken on responsibility for finance, HR and IT for all companies in their region. As mentioned in appendix 1, one could question whether training may become less product specific and hence dilute D plc's competences in these areas.*
  - *The figure of cutting direct costs by 10% seems very ambitious (or even unrealistic?) without further evidence to substantiate it. In chapter 3, one exercise will be to redraft the forecast with different figures for this.*
  - *Institutional investors may not be satisfied with the revenue growth assumptions (i.e. zero!) and may put pressure on the board to boost sales as well.*

Financing and cash flow

- *You could question whether the average cost of 8% will apply over the next 3 years, especially given problems in the Eurozone affecting credit ratings, although most commentators are expecting interest rates to stay low in an attempt to boost economies.*

- *Repaying £250m in 2015 could be problematic - this will be discussed further in chapter 3 under cash flow.*

D plc: Extract from published accounts

	2011	2010	2009	2008	2007
Completions					
Number of houses sold	9,673	9,582	11,798	15,383	16,152
Average sellling price					
£000 rounded	170	160	172	190	189
Revenue					
£ million	1,644.4	1,533.1	2,029.3	2,922.8	3,052.7
Profit from operations					
£ million	131.6	53.7	223.2	613.8	610.5
Operating margin	8.00%	3.50%	11.00%	21.00%	20.00%

Extract from Published Consolidated Income Statement of D plc for the
Year to 31 December 2011

	2011 £ million	2010 £ million
Revenue	1,644.4	1,533.1
Cost of sales	1,421.3	1,379.8
Gross profit	223.1	153.3
Operating expenses	91.5	99.6
Profit from operations	131.6	53.7
Finance costs	31.9	49.4
Profit before tax	99.7	4.3
Tax	27.9	1.2
Profit for year	71.8	3.1

Statement of Financial Position of D plc as at:

	Note	31.12.2011 £ million	£ million	31.12.2012 £ million	£ million
Assets					
Non-current assets					
Intangible assets	1	135.4		135.4	
Property, plant and equipment		20.5		33.1	
Total non-current assets			155.9		168.5
Current assets					
Inventories	2	2,021.2		2,131.8	
Trade and other receivables		48.4		49.6	
Cash and cash equivalents		112.8		124.2	
Total current assets			2,182.4		2,305.6
Total assets			2,338.3		2,474.1
Equity and liabilities					
Equity					
Ordinary share capital issued		25.0		25.0	
Share premium		150.0		150.0	
Retained earnings		1,179.3		1,107.5	
Total equity			1,354.3		1,282.5
Non-current liabilities					
Loans and borrowings	3	345.0		525.0	
Trade and other payables		132.5		83.9	
Total non-current liabilities			477.5		608.9
Current liabilities					
Loans and borrowings		55.0		121.6	
Trade and other payables		423.6		459.9	
Tax payable	4	27.9		1.2	
Total current liabilities			506.5		582.7
Total equity and liabilities			2,338.3		2,474.1

Notes to account extracts:

Note 1 Intangible assets

This consists of brand values and goodwill, which are reviewed annually in line with the relevant company procedures, which indicate that in 2011 there was no impairment to these values. The goodwill is allocated to strategic land holdings.

Note 2 Inventories

These consist of land, work in progress, part exchange properties and show houses.

All are considered to be current in nature although the operational cycle is such that a proportion will not be realised within 12 months.

Regular reviews are made to ascertain the net realisable value, and adjustments made when specific inventory is acquired and released as sales.

Note 3 Non-current liabilities (Loans and borrowings)

These consist of loan notes:

£250 million maturing 2015

£95 million maturing 2020

Both 8% nominal interest rate

Note 4 Tax payable

The corporation tax rate is 28%

Statement of Cash Flows for D plc for the year ended 31 December 2011

Cash flows from operating activities	£ million	£ million
Profit before tax		99.7
Adjustments		
Depreciation	4.7	
Finance costs	31.9	36.6
Movements in working capital		
(Increase)/decrease in inventories	110.6	
(Increase)/decrease in trade receivables	1.2	
Increase/(decrease) in trade payables	12.3	124.1
Cash generated from operations		260.4
Finance costs (net paid)	(31.9)	
Tax paid	(1.2)	(33.1)
Net cash from operating activities		227.3
Cash flows from investing activities		
Purchase of non-current assets	(2.0)	
Sale of non-current assets	9.9	7.9
Cash flows from financing activities		
Redemption of loans and borrowings		(246.6)
(Decrease)/increase in cash and cash equivalents		(11.4)
Cash and cash equivalents at beginning of year		124.2
Cash and cash equivalents at the end of the year		112.8

Forecast Income Statement for D plc taking account of the proposed 10% direct cost reduction (prepared prior to Annual General Meeting held in April 2012)

	2012 £ million	2013 £ million	2014 £ million
Revenue	**1,615.0**	**1,615.0**	**1,615.0**
Cost of sales	1,259.7	1,259.7	1,259.7
Gross Profit	**355.3**	**355.3**	**355.3**
Operating expenses	94.3	97.2	100.2
Profit from operations	261.0	258.1	255.1
Finance costs	31.9	31.9	31.9
Profit before tax	**229.1**	**226.2**	**223.2**
Tax	64.1	63.3	62.5
Profit for the year	**165.0**	**162.9**	**160.7**

Forecast Statement of Cash Flows for D plc taking account of the proposed 10% direct cost reduction (prepared prior to Annual General Meeting held in April 2012)

Cash flows from operating activities	2012 £ million		2013 £ million		2014 £ million	
Profit before tax		229.1		226.2		223.2
Adjustments						
Depreciation	4.7		4.7		4.7	
Finance costs	31.9	36.6	31.9	36.6	31.9	36.6
Movements in working capital		0		0		0
No significant movement expected						
Cash generated from operations		265.7		262.8		259.8
Finance costs (Net Paid)	(31.9)		(31.9)		(31.9)	
Tax paid	(27.9)	(59.8)	(64.1)	(96.0)	(63.3)	(95.2)
Net cash generated from operating activities		205.9		166.8		164.6
Cash flows from investing activities		0		0		0
No significant purchases or sales of non-current assets expected						
Cash flows from financing activities		0		0		0
Redemption of loans and borrowings – No redemptions of loans and borrowings expected		0		0		0
Cash and cash equivalents at beginning of year		112.8		318.7		485.5
Cash and cash equivalents at end of year		318.7		485.5		650.1
(Decrease)/increase in cash and cash equivalents		205.9		166.8		164.6

Cash flow is expected to remain positive in line with the steady state of predicted sales completions and planned cost reductions. No major fixed asset purchases or sales are planned. No significant movements in working capital are expected over the forecast period.

Strategic and financial analysis of the case material

Chapter learning objectives

By the end of this chapter you will:

- Have applied some key technical models from the strategic level to the current case material

- Know how to best utilise these models in the exam to gain marks

- Be aware of the most useful models to use in the exam given the current pre-seen material

How to use this chapter

To get the most out of this chapter, you should work through each exercise, applying each strategic model or tool to the pre-seen information. When you've completed each exercise you can check your attempt by using the suggested answers at the back of the chapter.

You should not attempt this chapter until you have read through the pre-seen material in detail and listened to the case analysis recording on EN-gage.

1 PESTEL

Usefulness in the exam

PESTEL issues are often key drivers of growth, decline and change within markets.

How to ensure you capture the marks

To score marks for using the PESTEL model you **don't** have to produce the whole model in an appendix. This will waste valuable time and result in you writing information that is not relevant to the point you're making. Instead you should consider doing an extract from the model, just highlighting the aspects you're referring to. Better still, you could just refer to the model in the body of your report, explaining the impact on revenue growth or margins. This way you cut down the risk of spending time on an appendix that you later forget to refer to.

Test your understanding 1 - PESTEL

Identify the key external influences in the industry using the PESTEL model:

Political	
Economic	
Social	
Technological	
Environmental	
Legal	

2 Porter's 5 forces

Usefulness in the exam

Porter's 5 forces is likely to be an easy model to apply in the exam. Situations in which it can be used include:

- discussing the high competitive rivalry in the industry

- considering barriers to entry if the unseen includes market development strategies (e.g. D plc expanding into Country Y or the threat from new entrants into the UK)

How to ensure you capture the marks

Similar to PESTEL, preparing a full appendix containing analysis of all of the five forces can waste valuable time, especially if you only apply the model briefly in your report. A better approach is to prepare an extract, highlighting the forces that are relevant or even just refer to the model in the body of your report, explaining the impact of the force on the company's margins.

Test your understanding 2 - Porter's 5 forces

Assess the industry using Porter's 5 forces:

Force	Your response
Competitive rivalry	
Threat of entry	
Supplier power	
Customer power	
Threat of substitutes	
Summary	

3 Porter's Value Chain

Usefulness in the exam

Given the importance of competitive strategy in the case, you may wish to look at the underlying cost and value drivers in more detail, using the value chain.

How to ensure you capture the marks

Performing a full value chain analysis will take up far too much time. A better approach is to prepare an extract, highlighting the value and cost drivers that are relevant or even just refer to the model in the body of your report, explaining the impact on the organisation's competitive strategy.

Test your understanding 3 - Porter's Value Chain

We do not have sufficient information to apply the value chain to D plc in detail. However, it would be worth considering the information we do have. Suggest possible factors that drive D plc's competitive advantage using Porter's Value Chain:

Primary Activities	Your response
Inbound logistics	
Operations	
Outbound logistics	
Marketing	
Service	
Support Activities	
Firm Infrastructure	
Human Resource Management	
Technology Development	
Procurement	

4 Porter's generic strategies

Usefulness in the exam

In a highly competitive industry it is vital that a firm has a clear, sustainable competitive advantage. Using Porter's generic strategy model forces you to consider a range of important issues in this case, such as economies of scale, brand strength and the significance of sustainability.

How to ensure you capture the marks

The easiest way to utilise Porter's generic strategies in the exam is to refer to model within the body of your report (rather than via an appendix). However, care must be taken to ensure you go into sufficient depth to earn both the technical and the application marks.

It is not good enough merely to state that the company operates a cost leadership or differentiation strategy. You must explain how they achieve this and things that might threaten their ability to maintain this (in which case this will lead to them becoming "stuck in the middle").

> ### Test your understanding 4 - Generic strategies
>
> Analyse how cost leadership, differentiation and focus can be used as competitive strategies in this industry in general and comment on the company's specific approach.

5 Financial statement analysis - historic information

Usefulness in the exam

In every case you are presented with financial statements and there is always scope to bring key ratios and trends into your discussion. In this case you have both historic and forecast results to assess (see later exercise on the forecasts).

How to ensure you capture the marks

Don't just say whether D plc's performance has got better or worse but try to discuss the reasons for any changes and/or the strategic implications of your findings.

Test your understanding 5 - Historic ratio analysis

Start by reviewing the ratios presented below and comment on how useful or relevant each of them might be:

Ratio	2011	Working	2010	Working	Comment
Revenue growth	7.24%	(1,644.4 ÷ 1,533.1)	24.45%	(2,029.3 - 1,533.1) ÷ 2,029.3	
% movement in house completions	0.95%	9,673 ÷ 9,582	18.78%	(11,798 – 9,582) ÷ 11,798	
% movement in average selling price	6.25%	170 ÷ 160	- 6.98%	(172 – 160) ÷ 172	
Gross profit margin	13.57%	223.1 ÷ 1,644.1	10.00%	153.3 ÷ 1,533.1	
Gross profit per completed house sold	£23,064	223.1 ÷ 9,673	27.6%	£15,999	
Interest cover	4.1 ×	131.6 ÷ 31.9	1.1 ×	53.7 ÷ 49.4	
ROCE	7.18%	131.6 / (1,354.3 + 477.5)	2.84%	53.7 / (1,282.5 + 608.9)	
Inventory holding period (in months)	17.06	2,021.2 ÷ 1,421.3 × 12	18.54	2,131.8 ÷ 1,379.8 × 12	
Receivables collection period (in months)	0.35	48.4 ÷ 1,644.4 × 12	0.39	49.6 ÷ 1,533.1 × 12	
Payables payment period (in months) - current only	3.58	423.6 ÷ 1,421.3 × 12	4.0	459.9 ÷ 1,379.8 × 12	

Cash operating cycle (in months)	13.83		14.93		
Gearing (debt ÷ equity)	0.25	345.0 ÷ 1,354.3	0.41	525 ÷1,282.5	

Now evaluate what these ratios (along with other figures from appendix 2) tell you so you can comment under the following headings.

Heading	Your response
Profitability	
Liquidity and working capital	
Investor ratios and gearing	

6 Mendelow's matrix

Usefulness in the exam

Mendelow's matrix is very often an easy technical model to include within your answer.

How to ensure you capture the marks

It is not good enough to merely state who different stakeholders are. You must ensure you expand your comment to cover the implications of your categorisation. So, for example, the organisation must ensure key players are included in any major changes in strategy.

Test your understanding 6 - Mendelow's matrix		
Assess the organisation's stakeholder relationships using Mendelow's matrix:		
	Low Interest	**High Interest**
Low Power		
High Power		

7 Critical success factors

Usefulness in the exam

An awareness of the critical success factors (CSFs) will be crucial to your ability to prioritise the issues as well as analyse potential solutions.

How to ensure you capture the marks

Similar to Porter's generic strategies, whenever you refer to a CSF you must clearly explain why it is a CSF and the nature of any potential threat to it (or indeed how a CSF may be strengthened by an opportunity).

Test your understanding 7 - CSFs

Identify the critical success factors in the industry and assess whether the organisation has the resources required to meet those CSFs.

CSF	Organisation

8 Identifying risks

Usefulness in the exam

Identifying the risks facing the organisation will help to reveal potential issues that could crop up in the unseen information, thereby allowing you to feel better prepared.

In addition, it will provide a greater awareness of the pressures facing the Board and will ensure you fully consider the implications of recommendations that you make.

It is therefore a useful background model but is not one you would normally have to reproduce in the exam.

Test your understanding 8 - Identifying risks

Identify the main risks facing the organisation using the following headings:

Question	Your response
Business risks	
Financial risks	
Political and legal risks	
Technology risk	
Economic risk	
Reputation risk	

9 Financial statement analysis - forecasts

Usefulness in the exam

In some cases you are presented with a set of forecasts to assess in the pre-seen material.

Often a key aspect in the exam will be to comment on the company's ability to achieve these forecasts given the issues it is facing. This will be easier if, prior to the exam, you have identified and evaluated the key assumptions made so to ensure you can identify the threats in the exam itself.

An understanding of how challenging (or not) the original forecast is will also help you assess the drive of the Board and how ambitious they are.

How to ensure you capture the marks

Don't just say whether D plc's forecast is likely to be achieved or not, discuss the reasons for your comments and/or the strategic implications of your findings.

Test your understanding 9 - Ratio analysis - Forecasts
Identify the key assumptions made in the forecast and comment on their reasonableness.

Test your understanding 10 - Revising the forecast

Using the template below, prepare a revised forecast for 2012 showing the impact if the reduction in direct costs was not at the forecast level of 10%. Comment on the results.

Your response

Cut in direct costs	*0%*	*5%*	*8%*
Income statement			
Revenue	1,615.0	1,615.0	1,615.0
Cost of sales			
Gross profit			
Operating expenses	94.3	94.3	94.3
Profit from operations			
Finance costs	31.9	31.9	31.9
Profit before tax			
Tax			
Revised Profit for the year			
Cash generated from operations as forecast	265.7	265.7	265.7
Adjustment required due to the above			
Revised cash generated from operations			

10 Balanced scorecard

Usefulness in the exam

Balanced scorecard is likely to be an easy model to apply in this exam. Situations in which it can be used include:

- looking at developing management information systems and KPIs in the context of a wider balanced scorecard approach.

- as part of the recommendations section regarding proposed strategies - a balanced scorecard could be part of the control systems set up to manage a new venture.

How to ensure you capture the marks

More often than not, the balanced scorecard will be part of the recommendations you are giving to the Board. As such, examples of specific KPIs for each of the four perspectives must be given to convey the benefits of such an approach. One or two examples under each perspective is more than enough.

Test your understanding 11 - Balanced scorecard	
Question	**Your response**
Give some KPIs that could be used as part of a balanced scorecard analysis for D plc.	
Financial perspective	
Customer perspective	
Internal perspective	
Innovation and learning perspective	

11 Ansoff's matrix

Usefulness in the exam

This should prove to be a very useful model for this case and one where easy marks can be obtained. The majority of strategies that may have to be evaluated in the exam will fit into Ansoff's matrix.

How to ensure you capture the marks

The problem often experienced when using Ansoff's within the case study exam is ensuring you do *apply* the model rather than just making statements like "this would be classified as product development" which leave the reader asking the question "so what?!"

To apply Ansoff's to your issue you need to focus your argument on risk and the key factors to ensure the success of that strategy. So for example you could comment that:

*   A product development strategy (or market development strategy) would result in additional risk for the company over and above a market penetration strategy

*   A market development strategy will be more successful the closer the characteristics of the new markets are to existing markets

*   When following a product development strategy success will only be achieved if the new product satisfies the critical success factors required in existing markets.

Test your understanding 12 - Ansoff's matrix

Assess directions for strategic growth using Ansoff's matrix:

	Existing products	New products
Existing Markets		
New Markets		

12 Porter's Diamond

Usefulness in the exam

Porter developed his "Diamond" model to help analyse why certain nations are more competitive than others and why some industries within nations are more competitive than others. However, it is also used as part of an assessment of the attactiveness of a particular country for investment. To get this perspective, however, is not always easy.

Situations in which it can be used include:

- If D plc expands into Country Y , then will the incumbent domestic firms be particularly competitive, due to them having been based in Country Y?

- Will D plc have an inherent advantage over firms in Y , simply because it comes from the UK?

How to ensure you capture the marks

Ensure that any use of the model is linked back to the key question being discussed - e.g. should D plc invest in Country Y and. if so, how?

Test your understanding 13 - Porter's Diamond

Assess any potential expansion into Country Y using Porter's Diamond model (obviously there are many points that the model does not address. Here, try to limit your discussion to issues raised by the model)

Factor conditions	
Demand Conditions	
Related and supporting industries	
Firm strategy, structure and rivalry	

13 Financing

Usefulness in the exam

When analysing any issue and making recommendations, it is important that you address the impact on cash. This may mean that the organisation needs to access further cash, in which case you would be expected to assess how much cash is required and to think about likely sources.

Test your understanding 14 - Financing

Comment on the historic, current and future financing of the organisation.

Your response

14 Valuation of a business

Usefulness in the exam

An appreciation of the different methods of valuing an organisation in this industry could prove useful if the un-seen material asks you to consider future acquisitions.

The key is to keep your calculations simple on the day and clearly state any assumptions made.

Test your understanding 15 - Valuing the organisation

Question

Discuss how you would value a business in this industry. Your response should include a range of valuation methods and calculations (where possible) and should consider the suitability of methods, possible difficulties, etc.

Your response

15 Net Present Value (NPV)

Usefulness in the exam

Discounted cash flows (especially NPV) allow you to assess the impact of future plans on shareholder value. This is particularly useful for

- Evaluating a strategy - e.g. expanding into a new country

- Business valuation - e.g further growth through acquisition

How to ensure you capture the marks

Most students are happy setting out their workings in an appendix but to capture all the marks it is imperative that you:

- State any assumptions you have made regarding figures used - e.g. growth forecasts, choice of discount rate used.

- Refer to the answer in your report, cross referencing.

- Use the figure as part of your analysis, arguments or recommendations. You need to "make the numbers talk". For example, if a NPV is positive then this can be incorporated into a discussion of "acceptability" when assessing a strategy. You can often pick up judgement marks by commenting where a decision might be marginal or, if appropriate, by comparing two NPVs against each other.

- Ensure the numbers are balanced by non-financial considerations as well.

Test your understanding 16 - NPV

Recap of some basic techniques

(a) Suppose you are looking at an investment in Country Y.

Suppose further it uses the Y$ as its currency and the current spot rate is £1 = Y$2. Inflation rates are expected to be 3% in the UK and 15% in Country Y.

Calculate the exchange rate in two years time.

(b) Suppose D plc is considering an investment that requires the purchase of some plant and equipment on the 1st January 2013. When would the first tax savings arising from capital allowances occur, assuming tax is paid one year after the end of the accounting period?

(c) Suppose the examiner tells you to use a ten year planning horizon and the cash flows from t_4 to t_{10} are constant. If the discount rate is 10%, what is the discount factor that should used on this annuity?

(d) Suppose instead you are discounting cash flows into infinity and that the cash flows have constant growth of 3% from t_4 onwards. If the cash flow at t_4 is £25m, what is the present value of the cash flows from t_4 to infinity? The discount rate is still 10%.

(e) If discounting project cash flows, would you include interest payments?

Test your understanding answers

Test your understanding 1 - PESTEL	
Political	• Government policies on the use of greenfield v brownfield sites and any assistance given to help with the latter. • Government policy on the use of greenbelt land • Government target that all new builds will be carbon neutral by 2016 • Government targets for the number of new houses to be built and where • Local government impact on gaining planning permission and the inevitable delays involved
Economic	• The state of the building industry and the demand for new houses in particular is closely linked to the state of the economy (i.e. high systematic risk) • Interest rates directly impact the cost of mortgages and hence demand for housing • The credit crisis still means that it is harder to borrow funds - this affects both the building companies and their ultimate customers • Unemployment and fear of losing a job will also affect demand • Growth in other countries will create opportunities (e.g. Country Y)
Social	• In the UK most people expect to own their own home at some point in their lives • The mix of demand for large family houses v smaller single person dwellings will be affected by divorce rates, the age mix of the population, etc • People living longer / increase in second home ownership could also affect the supply of second hand housing and hence the demand for new builds. • Convergence of tastes will create opportunities (e.g. Country Y)

Technological	• MMC
	• Design software makes it easier to design houses
	• Supply chain management and project management software should make it easier to control processes
Environmental	• Global warming, climate change and increased flooding impact location of new builds and the nature of designs.
	• Pressure for more energy efficient houses and for increased use of renewable materials (such as wood)
Legal	• Localism Act in UK - gives more power to local communities to influence planning decisions
	• Planning laws and regulations
	• Legislation on energy efficiency - e.g. on the use of insulation in properties

In summary, the key issues are:

- The state of the economy

- The cost and availability of finance

- Government policies on planning

The above issues combined would suggest that in the short-term there is limited growth opportunities within the UK house-building market.

Test your understanding 2 - Porter's 5 forces

Force	Your response
Competitive rivalry	High competitive rivalry in the UK due to • Large number of players of different sizes. • Low overall growth in the industry • Difficult to differentiate products, except perhaps through energy efficiency and use of MMC • Limited availability of suitable land resulting in greater competition to acquire it in the first place. Rivalry may be lower in other markets.
Threat of entry	The barriers to entry include the following: • Brand strength of incumbent firms • Expertise of incumbent firms in understanding local markets (most other expertise is bought in) • Developing a good relationship with planning offices • Capital requirements are fairly low - construction is labour intensive and most equipment can be hired if necessary Overall these barriers are fairly weak resulting in a high threat of entry, as witnessed by firms entering the UK from continental Europe.

Supplier power	Low for materials and labour
	• numerous sub-contrcators available for labour
	• numerous suppliers of bulding materials, undifferentiated products
	Power of suppliers higher for land
	• Suppliers of prime land sites are in a strong position
	• Local planning office has very high power
Customer power	Low
	• While individual customers have little purchasing power, the wide availability of choice and the lack of differentiation of products makes it difficult to tie them in
Threat of substitutes	High
	• Main threat is second hand property available for rent or purchase
	• Lot of property available but high prices in some parts of the country make new property more attractive. (However this will partly be offset by higher land prices in such areas)
Summary	High competitive rivalry and acquiring land (incorporating the power of planning offices) are key determinants of profitability

Test your understanding 3 - Porter's Value Chain

Primary Activities	Your response
Inbound logistics	• This refers to the choice of suppliers / sub-contractors and the acquisition of land. • The NED NN has suggested that there is a problem regarding the source of supplies but we are not told what it may relate to...yet. • This category can also refer to storage and handling of raw materials. Given the costs of transportation and storage D plc will only buy materials when it needs them and then from local suppliers. There might be some issues relating to on-site storage (e.g. theft) but we are not told about this.
Operations	• This refers to design and building of houses • Local expertise and knowledge will ensure houses are designed that closely match customer needs • Given D plc outsources much of its supply chain, we need to consider what exactly D plc does to create a competitive advantage. For example, D plc is unlikely to gain sustainable advantages when using sub-contractors or in the purchase of materials • There is definitely scope to improve the energy efficiency and carbon neutrality of houses by the greater use of MMC
Outbound logistics	• Doesn't really apply in this case.
Marketing	• We are not told much about D plc's sales and marketing functions, except that there are 9 individual centres doing this for their own business units and regions, suggesting a high degree of local focus but duplication of effort and a lack of standardisation.
Service	• In the UK builders have to give a 10 year guarantee on new properties. We are not told of any problems or successes for D plc in this respect.

Support Activities	Your response
Firm Infrastructure	• You could argue that D plc's organisational structure is complex with repetition of tasks. This will result in missed opportunities for centralised bulk puchasing and other cost savings. • Furthermore the strategic planning process seems overly formal and rigid, reducing the firm's flexibility to respond to market conditions.
Human Resource Management	• We are told little about staff training and development to enhance core competences other than the NED NN sees it as a problem
Technology Development	• D plc has fialed to integrate IT systems from the different businesses it has acquired. • D plc has failed to embrace MMC
Procurement	• Issues relating to suppliers have been covered under "inbound logistics" above.

Note: we are also told that "D plc has threshold competences in most areas of its value chain activities"

Test your understanding 4 - Generic strategies

Application of Porter's generic strategies model to the house building industry:

Cost-leadership

- Purchasing economies of scale may be available to larger firms (e.g. in buying bricks) but the high cost of transportation will mean that local suppliers may be preferred, limiting the potential for quantity discounts.

- Most labour is sub-contracted so it is difficult to see where cost advantages could arise, unless larger firms can exercise bargaining power to drive down sub-contractor rates.

- Larger firms may benefit from being able to buy larger plots of land to build high numbers of houses if this then means the average land cost per house works out lower.

- Larger firms may have cost advantages from having specialist teams to deal with the planning process.

- Larger firms may be able to make use of project management tools such as critical path analysis to improve the efficiency of the build process on larger projects.

While the above will result in some advantages to larger firms, there still seems to be room for many smaller operators in the industry as well.

Differentiation

There are a number of ways that companies can try to differentiate their products and so charge higher prices, including

- Developing a brand synonymous with high quality, although it is debatable how effective this is

- Greater knowledge of local markets and trends allows builders to make houses that are closer to what customers want

- Innovative designs and features

- Use of superior materials (e.g. marble floors)

- Greater energy efficiency

- Simply building larger houses with more land, etc, aimed at more wealthy customers

Most of the above can be replicated by rivals if they chose to do so.

Focus

- Some firms specialise in niche segments - e.g. luxury executive housing, houses that look like barn conversions, etc

The company - D plc

D has three sub units (H, R and S) focussing on different market segments and claims to have core competences in its knowledge of local markets. Whether this is sufficient to gain a **sustainable** competitive advantage going forwards is debatable as presumably rivals can gain local knowledge if they choose to do so.

Together with government plans over new houses being carbon neutral, D plc should consider a greater emphasis on MMC.

Test your understanding 5 - Historic ratio analysis

Your comments on the usefulness or relevance of the ratios calculated may have included:

- ROCE is difficult to assess due to the definition of 'capital employed'. In particular, the long-term trade and other payables (should these be regarded as long-term capital employed) and the short-term loan and borrowings (it's unclear what these are)

- The cash operating cycle elements are potentially misleading due to the treatment of land. In particular, trade payables where we have both long-term (ignored within our calculations) and short-term. A review of other housebuilders accounts suggest that long-term trade payables often relate to land payables.

- The gearing calculation has to be based on book values (since that is all we have). Market values would provide a more current assessment. Similar issues as for ROCE when it comes to assessing what is classified as debt

It is important to be aware of these comments when interpretting the ratios.

Heading	Your response
Profitability	Sales • Sales up by 7.26% in 2011, which is impressive in the current recession and is finally an increase after four years of decline. However, total sales are still significantly lower than in 2009 and before and we are told a competitor has done better. • The number of completions is only up by 0.95% but this is still good given the steady decline in numbers from 2007 to 2010. We are told that completion volumes are unlikely to grow over the next 3 years. • The main reason for higher sales is the fact that the average selling price is up 6.25% from £160,000 to £170,000, nearly back to 2009 levels. • The increase in average price is due to a change in sales mix towards more expensive properties, especially in the Eastern region. However, no future change in mix is anticipated meaning that unless property prices grow generally, there is no increase in sales revenue expected. You could question why such improvements in mix couldn't be achieved in the Northern and Central regions as well. Operating profit and margins • Operating profit has increased by 145% from £53.7m to £131.6m, a much greater growth than that for sales revenue. However, it is still substantially lower than in the period 2007 to 2009. • Operating margins have increased from 3.5% to 8.0% due to an 8% cut in operating expenses. While this is an improvement there is still a long way to go to get the 20% margins that were typical before the impact of the credit crisis. • Going forwards there is little scope for further cuts to operating costs so D plc is looking at cutting direct costs to boost profits. This is discussed further under forecasts below but it raises the concern that the quality of properties could be eroded if costs are cut too drastically.

Heading	Your response
Profitability (cont'd)	Return on capital employed • ROCE (including all non-current liabilities in capital employed) has increased from 2.84% to 7.18%, due mainly to the increase in operating profit. Profit for the year • Profit for the year has increased from £3.1m to £71.8m, which would be warmly welcomed by institutional shareholders, unless of course they expected better!
Liquidity and working capital	Working capital and liquidity present a mixed picture. • Inventory holding period has fallen from 18.5 to 17.1 months (note: you could use days and stated that the holding period has fallen from 564 to 519 days). You could view this as a positive - D plc are reducing their risk exposure - or negative - D plc are running down their landbank to boost short term cash flow at the expense of longer term profitability. • Receivables days are down slightly from 0.39 months to 0.35 months (12 days to 11 days) but this is not an area of concern for D plc as customers generally get mortgages to pay for houses so the builder will always get their money very quickly. • Payables days are down from 4 months to 3.58 months (122 days to 109 days). This could bring additional strain to cash flow but this is unlikely to be significant. . • The cash operating cycle has fallen from 14.93 months to 13.83 (454 (564 + 12 - 122) to 421 days (519 + 11 - 109)). • Quick and current ratios cannot really be calculated here as we do not have a split between land expected to be sold within one year and after one year. • The net movement in working capital resulted in an extra £124.1m cash in 2011

Heading	Your response
Investor ratios and gearing	• Gearing (measured as debt/equity and using non-current loans only and book values) has fallen from 0.41 to 0.25. Given current uncertainty in the housing market and fears over financing, you could argue that reducing gearing risk is a wise move. However, you could also see this as a symptom of an unambitious board who are not investing for growth. • Interest cover has improved from 1.09 to 4.1, which would certainly encourage the banks • We do not have sufficient information to comment on movements in the share price, dividend yield and dividend cover

Note: the above discussion is mainly based on comparing 2010 and 2011. Ideally we would compare D plc with other firms and/or industry averages.

	Low Interest	**High Interest**
Low Power	• General public. • Activist groups will monitor environmental credentials of the larger firms like D plc. However, if a problem arises, then activists may become more interested and acquire power through working with media channels. • Individual shareholders	• Smaller sub-contractors • Employees • Most customers
High Power	• Banks as long as D plc meets its interest payments and doesn't exceed its overdraft limit the banks should be kept happy. However, should either of these look as if they will be compromised, then expect an active involvement! • Government bodies concerned with regulation or safety legislation concerning the building industry. • Institutional shareholders.	• Planning authorities. • (Directors - obviously they have high power and interest but are not really relevant to the discussion here unless you get a split between different groups of directors)

In summary key relationships that need to be managed are:

• Planning authorities

• Banks

• Institutional shareholders

Test your understanding 7 - CSFs

CSFs (usually derived by looking at the market)	Organisational competencies
Land purchasing • Right place • Right price • Right time Whether to buy 'strategic' land or 'short-term' (more expensive).	• We are not given sufficient information to assess whether or not D plc has strengths or weaknesses in this area. • D does manage an extensive land bank with average stock holding period of 17.1 months for 2011. Reduced from 18.5 months in 2010, D is trying to reduce is risk exposure in this area.
Getting planning permission and managing the planning process effectively. This includes converting strategic land to short term land, and the speed of the building development. Finishing developments on time for customer who buy 'off plan'.	• We are not given sufficient information to assess whether or not D plc has strengths or weaknesses in this area. • Property completions increased by 0.95% to 9,673 in 2011.
Reputation for Quality of housing this includes; • house spec • lifestyle homes • storage space, driveways, gardens • outdoor space • right mix of housing on a development	• D has a good reputation for houses in all of their brands. • One of D's aims is 'to continue to build quality homes that customers buy' so is aware of the importance of this.

Branding	• By having H, R and S brands, this covers a large proportion of the housing market in the UK. • D is still known as a 'major player in the premier league of house-building'.
Pricing of houses incorporating value for money.	• House prices increased by 6.25% in 2011 to £170,000. Each region has varying average selling prices, so this is monitored closely.
Cash flow management, especially given the long operating cycle involved with managing land banks.	• D plc generated £227.3m of cash from ordinary operations in 2011. However, it used more than this in repaying loans, a cause for concern.
Managing sub-contractors • Reviewing quality of work performed • Efficiency • Remedial work for snagging issues	• Cutting costs during 2011, and hoping for a further cost cutting programme in 2012 may cause some issues in this area.

Test your understanding 8 - Identifying risks

Question	Your response
Business risks	• Competitive rivalry - D plc has not performed as well as a leading competitor • Difficulties acquiring suitable land in the right place at the right price • Misjudging the market and making houses people do not want to buy • Not responding quickly enough to market changes due to inflexibility • Failure to invest in MMC
Financial risks	• FX risks if expand overseas • Interest rate risk on loans • Working capital and cash flow management
Political and legal risks	• Failure to meet UK government targets for carbon neutral housing by 2016 • Changes in legislation re planning law, access to brownfield or greenfield sites, etc • Changes in legislation re house designs - energy efficiency, insulation, mix of social housing • Political instability in Country Y if decide to expand there
Technology risk	• Failure to incorporate MMC • Failure to incorporate other energy efficient and renewable energy technologies • Failure to integrate IT systems between divisions

Economic risk	• Economic recession has a major impact on house demand • Higher interest rates could dampen demand for new houses.
Reputation risk	• Protests and bad publicity over projects

Test your understanding 9 - Ratio analysis - Forecasts

Your response

- No change in sales revenue, the number of completions, average selling price or mix
    - The potential move into Country Y has been excluded
    - In November 2011 the Office for Budget Responsibility (OBR) in the UK forecast that for the whole UK property market the number of transactions would fall by 3% in 2011/12 before increasing by 1.5% in 2012/13 and 20.7% in 2013/14. Furthermore it predicted that the average house price would fall by 0.9% in 2011/12 and by 0.1% in 2012/13 before increasing by 2.7% in 2013/14. Even if you argue for a fairly neutral net result in 2011/12 and 2012/13, the figures would suggest a more major improvement in 2013/14.

- 10% cut in direct costs
    - Presumably this comes from centralising procurement and other operational changes
    - We have little evidence upon which to evaluate this claim, except that an 8% cut was achieved in overheads in 2011.
    - The main danger here is the build quality will be compromised in some way.

- Operating costs to grow at 3% per annum
    - Reasonable given forecast inflation rates in the UK

- Additions to and usage of the land bank to be neutral.

    - Reasonable

- No reduction in loans
  - This is surprising given that we have £55m of loans shown on the statement of financial position at 31.12.11 as "current liabilities" so presumably would be repaid in 2012. It may be that this represents an overdraft but we do not know for certain.

- No major non-current asset purchases
  - Unambitious.
  - We do not know the detail of the non-current assets held but presumably some plant and equipment will need replacing?

- No changes in net working capital
  - Reasonable given the assumptions concerning sales and the number of completions

Key implications of the figures produced

- Based on the above assumptions operating profit will increase by 98% from 2011 to 2012

- It will then fall over the next two years by an average of 1% each year.

- Despite the increase in operating profit, cash generated from operating activities will fall from £260.4m in 2011 to £205.9m and will fall thereafter. It would be interesting to see what the figures would look like if the 10% cut in costs does not materialise (see next TYU)

- However, overall it looks like D plc will be able to accumulate cash resulting in £650.1m for 2015, enough to redeem the 2015 loan notes.

Conclusion

- You could argue that the forecasts are too conservative and that the board seem unprepared to take risks to grow the business.

- The plan gives a benefit in the next year but steady decline thereafter. Is this evidence of a very short-termist view?

- You could argue that the forecasts have been manipulated simply to make 2012 cash flow look better.

- Institutional shareholders may be unimpressed!

Note: if given some management accounts for part of 2012, use them to assess whether or not the plan is working.

Test your understanding 10 - Revising the forecast

Cut in direct costs	0%	5%	8%
Income statement			
Revenue	1,615.0	1,615.0	1,615.0
Cost of sales (W1)	1,400.0	1,330.0	1,288.0
Gross profit	215.0	285.0	327.0
Operating expenses	94.3	94.3	94.3
Profit from operations	120.7	190.7	232.7
Finance costs	31.9	31.9	31.9
Profit before tax	**88.8**	**158.8**	**200.8**
Tax	24.9	44.5	56.2
Revised Profit for the year	**63.9**	**114.3**	**144.6**
Cash generated from operations as forecast	265.7	265.7	265.7
Adjustment required due to the above (W2)	(140.3)	(70.3)	(28.3)
Revised cash generated from operations	**125.4**	**195.4**	**237.4**

W1: Cost estimate of 1,259.7 is after savings of 10%, so the gross figure would be 1,259.7 / 0.9 = 1,400

W2: e.g. for 0% estimate the difference in profit before tax is 88.8 v 229.1, ie a fall of 140.3. The difference in tax would not impact cash flow until a year later, so would be relevant for 2013.

Comments

The savings estimate has a significant impact on the 2012 forecasts so should be highlighted as a key figure for sensitivity analysis.

Test your understanding 11 - Balanced scorecard

Question	Your response
Financial perspective	• Revenue • Forward sales • Operating margin • Profit before tax • Gearing • Free cash flow generated • ROCE • Net assets per share • Share price
Customer perspective	• Customer satisfaction surveys - what % of customers would recommend D plc to a friend? • Most new homes in the UK are protected by the National House-Building Council (NHBC) 10-year Buildmark warranty and insurance. Presumably D plc do this or offer a similar guarantee. The number of claims received on new houses under the scheme should be monitored. • Number of affordable homes completed, both in total and as a percentage of total homes built.

Internal perspective	• Number of housing completions
	• Number of reportable injuries on site
	• Number of health and safety prosecutions
	• Size of the land bank (e.g. number of plots) with and without planning permission
	• Total carbon emissions (tonnes)
	• Number of sustainable houses built
	• Waste generated in total and per house sold
	• % of waste recycled
	• Total waste taken to landfill
	• % of builds on brownfield sites
	• Number of trees planted, in total and per house
Innovation and learning perspective	• Number of training days provided, in total and per employee
	• Number of trainees and apprentices, in total and as a percentage of total employees
	• % of total houses that are carbon neutral
	• % of total houses that incorporated MMC
	• Average energy efficiency of new houses built (e.g. houses in the UK receive a SAP energy rating - innovation could be reflected in a better rating)

Test your understanding 12 - Ansoff's matrix

	Existing products	New products
Existing Markets	• Continue to build houses along the same lines as we have always done. (This seems to be the view of the Board!) • Make houses more energy efficient • Make houses that are carbon neutral. • Further acquisition of competitors • Pricing policy (reduced pricing, more part-ex deals etc)	• Make houses using MMC. • Switch to "investor" and/or "RSL" models
New Markets	• Expand into more regions within the UK - e.g.South West • Develop into new countries - e.g. Country Y	• Build commercial property such as offices • Vertical integration could include buying sub-contractors to reduce costs, employing more staff inhouse to avoid the use of sub-contractors and forwards integration into estate agents.

Test your understanding 13 - Porter's Diamond

Factor conditions	There is nothing to suggest that there are particular skills or natural resources within Y to give domestic firms an advantage in terms of UK housing styles, although there may be expertise in timber framed buildings. (As a comparison, one reason given for the global success of Swedish furniture companies is the abundance of wood as a building material and the development of skills in woodworking). One area where domestic builders will have developed expertise is in building houses that can withstand earthquakes and typhoons. This could indicate that D plc would have a disadvantage over domestic firms in this respect.
Demand Conditions	The growing affluence and influence of the middle classes may have forced some firms to develop high quality designs or processes to win buyers but if demand has outstripped supply then this would be less of a factor. As above, there is little here to concern D plc about the demand from customers in Y.
Related and supporting industries	We are not told much about supporting and related industries in Y and their impact on the competitive advantage of house builders.
Firm strategy, structure and rivalry	The growth and expansion of many building companies within Y suggests that there is a level of competition within the market. However, rapid growth in demand will have allowed many domestic firms to grow without having to hone their competitive edge.

In conclusion the main concern is the lack of expertise that D plc has in respect of incorporating earthquakes and typhoons into its design and build processes. Other than this, there is little indication that domestic firms will have an inherent advantage.

Test your understanding 14 - Financing

Financing to date

- Listed in 1982 but we are told little about financing before then.
- Similarly we are told little about how acquisitions were financed

Current position

- Long term loans of £345m at 31/12/11, giving gearing (as measured by debt/equity finance using non-current loans and book values) of 345/1,354.3 = 0.25 which seem reasonable (interest cover is 4.1)

- Cash was used in 2011 to repay £246.6m of loans, thus reducing gearing from 0.41 in 2010. Given current uncertainty in the housing market and fears over financing, you could argue that reducing gearing risk is a wise move. However, you could also see this as a symptom of an unambitious board who are not investing for growth.

Future financing - including the 3 year forecast

Debt solutions

We are told D plc has "always had good working relationships with its bankers and financial instututions". It should be able to raise further debt, especially as it had an additional £180m of long term loans in 2010 with effectively the same asset base to use as security.

D plc needs to redeem (and possibly refinance) £250m of debt in 2015. According to the cash forecasts in appendix 2 it should have sufficient cash to do this.

Equity solutions.

The lack of growth prospects and the zero dividend in 2011 will make investors very reluctant to buy further equity. Even a rights issue would need some major expansion plans to instill confidence.

Other

Other than looking at reducing the size of the land bank, better control of working capital would not make a significant impact on future cash flow. However, running down the land bank may be seen as being too short-termist and lacking a long term strategy.

Test your understanding 15 - Valuing the organisation

Market capitalisation

Given D plc is listed, we can use a share price for sales of minority stakes.

We could also use the share price to derive a market capitalisation but recognise that a premium would still have to be added should D plc be subject to a takeover bid.

Asset based approaches

At 31/12/11 the book value of D plc's shares was £1,354.3m. We are not told either the nominal value of shares nor the number of shares, so cannot deduce a price per share.

You could argue that an asset approach is useful for D plc for the following reasons:

- The bulk of the asset value is the land bank (included in inventories) where regular reviews are made of NRV and adjustments made if necessary.
- Brand values may be reflected in the intangible assets.

Earnings approaches

Basic idea is MV = P/E × future sustainable earnings

P/E ratio

Given D plc is listed we should be able to find its P/E ratio (presumably this would be given in the unseen) and then use it to value a potential acquistion, say.

If a target company is unquoted, then it is conventional to discount the P/E ratio by between 1/4 and 1/3 to reflect the lack of marketability of the unquoted shares, etc

Earnings

The P/E ratio given may be based on D plc's historic earnings or on forecast earnings. Either way, the key when using it is to ensure you apply it to the same type of earnings (historic v forecast).

A big advantage of this approach is that synergy could be incorporated into the earnings figures used. Note that "earnings" here is profit after tax, so remember to adjust for tax.

Present value of free cash flows

The idea here is to discount after tax operating cash flows at the company WACC and then deduct the value of debt to leave the value of equity. From a theoretical perspective this is a very powerful method, albeit often trickier than the methods mentioned above.

WACC

Calculating a WACC will be difficult without further information.

To get a cost of equity there are two commonly used approaches:

- DVM - e.g. $P = D_1 / (k_e - g)$ - we do not know the share price and it will tricky to estimate a dividend growth rate, given there was no dividend paid this year

- CAPM - this is more feasible in the exam but the unseen would have to contain data concerning a suitable beta, the risk free rate and the return on the market portfolio.

To get a cost of debt we could use the information given that we currently have £345m of long-term debt (plus £55m of short-term debt) with an 8% nominal interest rate.

To pull these together into a WACC would need the MV of both debt and equity. While a book value will suffice for the debt pushed, we really need the MV of the shares to calculate the WACC.

Cash flows

If valuing an acquisition , then we would need the cash flows of the target. However in some cases we might want to value the new combined entity in which case we would start with the predicted cash flows for D plc for the next 3 years and adjust them for the following:

- revisions to expected direct cost savings

- new projects / strategies (e.g. expansion in Country Y)

- synergies from acquisitions

Test your understanding 16 - NPV

Recap of some basic techniques

(a) Using purchasing power parity

Discount rate in one year = 2 × 1.15/1.03 = 2.233

Discount rate in two years = 2.233 × 1.15/1.03 = 2.493

(b) If we set 1st January 2013 as t=0, then the asset is bought in the y/e t_1 with tax being paid (and hence tax savings) at t_2.

(c) AF(4-10) = AF(1-10) - AF(1-3) = 6.145 - 2.487 = 3.658

(d) Value at t_3 = CF_4/(k-g) = 25/0.07 = 357.1m. PV = 357.1 × 0.751 = 268.2

(e) No, because the cost of finance is already included in the discount rate used.

Ethical considerations

Chapter learning objectives

By the end of this chapter you will:

- Be aware of the sustainability and ethical issues facing D plc
- Have considered what ethical issues face other firms in the building industry

1 Identifying ethical issues

Usefulness in the exam

Ethics, sustainability and CSR are potentially major issues for D plc.

Although you will be presented with new ethical issues to deal with in the unseen information, an understanding of those given in the pre-seen may help to provide a safety cushion in the exam.

Remember, to score highly in your ethics section you must explain the ethical dimension to the issue as well as provide clear recommendations.

Test your understanding 1 - Ethical issues	
Question	**Your response**
Comment on corporate governance within D plc	
Are there any areas of dubious business ethics that can be identified from the pre-seen?	
Are there any areas of questionable personal ethical behaviour for anyone mentioned in the pre-seen?	
What CSR / sustainability issues face firms in the building industry?	

Test your understanding answers

Test your understanding 1 - Ethical issues

Question	Your response
Comment on corporate governance within D plc	• Roles of chairman and CEO have been separated.
	• There are 4 NEDs indicating commitment to comply with governance best practice. Also NN's comments would indicate that the NEDs take their role of challenging the executive directors seriously.
	• No information given regarding audit or remuneration committees, although we would expect them to be present given D plc is listed on the London Stock Exchange.
	• The annual schedule of matters does include a section on risk monitoring.
	• Poor integration of IT systems could be seen as a weakness in the control system.
	• If D plc moves into Country Y then the difference in governance standards and how D plc manages this could be a concern.

Are there any areas of dubious business ethics that can be identified from the pre-seen?	Nothing given in the case that relates to D plc specifically. Areas to watch out for could include the following. Country Y • D plc may be tempted to adopt local standards re governance and social responsibility (or health and safety standards perhaps). • D plc employees may be tempted to indulge in bribery and corruption to win orders and gain planning consent.
Are there any areas of questionable personal ethical behaviour for anyone mentioned in the pre-seen?	The most obvious area of concern is the role of the Sales Director in suggesting Country Y as a possible area for expansion. Is his advice motivated by a desire to increase the wealth of D plc shareholders or to benefit his family or himself. It would be wise to limit his involvement to that of advice but for other board members to make the decision. Other areas to watch out for could include the following. • As mentioned above, in Country Y, D plc employees may be tempted to indulge in bribery and corruption to win orders and gain planning consent

What CSR / sustainability issues face firms in the building industry?	Land choice • Using greenfield (or even greenbelt) land for building is not sustainable. Repurposing brownfield sites is much better. The impact on the wider community • Building firms need to think more broadly about the impact on the environment and communities around developments. • This could include incorporating green parks into designs, planting trees, investing in local infrastructure (roads, schools, community centres, etc) • There is also an ethical issue over whether all houses are targeted at richer customers or whether affordable (social) houses are also included in a development.

What CSR / sustainability issues face firms in the building industry? (cont'd)	House design

	• The key sustainability point is the energy efficiency of houses being built. Houses last for many years and throughout their lifetime and occupation they will have a considerable environmental impact, particularly through the energy used to heat, light and power them.
	
	• Linked to this could be the incorporation of renewable energy sources, such as solar power or wind turbines, into designs.
	
	• The carbon impact of house design even impacts the choice of materials used:
	  – Wood is a more renewable source than, say, steel and concrete
	  – Are materials sourced locally to reduce transportation?
	
	Building process
	
	• Working with subcontractors to ensure waste is recycled rather than sent to landfill.
	
	Employees
	
	• Creating a supportive, enjoyable workplace & treating employees with respect.
	
	• Equal employment opportunities, no discrimination, developing employees, etc.
	
	• This can be a real challenge if much of the work is done by sub-contractors.

5

Key issues and options

Chapter learning objectives

By the end of this chapter you will:

- Consolidated your strategic and financial analysis by applying the SWOT analysis model to the current case material
- Have prioritised the SWOT, with justification
- Have linked these points together to come up with a shortlist of the key issues facing D plc.
- Have considered possible courses of action for each of these key issues.

1 SWOT

Usefulness in the exam

Your SWOT analysis should drive your prioritisations and as such, it is a key model.

How to ensure you capture the marks

You should always have a SWOT analysis as the first appendix of your report. You must make sure that it contains all of the issues that appear in the unseen (in many cases this can be achieved by ensuring all of the bold headings from the unseen are in your SWOT). It is also good if you include a couple of issues from the pre-seen. The examiner is often very critical if students don't fully update their SWOT analysis for the new information presented on the day.

Don't go over the top. You haven't got time to give lots of background information on each of the points you make. Neither have you got time to list 10 strengths, weaknesses etc. Try to aim for 3 or 4 points under each heading (although be prepared to be flexible where necessary)

Finally, after investing all the hard work preparing the appendix, you must remember to refer to it in the body of your report. The easiest place to do this is in your prioritisation section. As an opening sentence you can say:

"The following issues have been prioritised based on the SWOT analysis contained in appendix A".

Another excellent place to refer to your SWOT analysis is in your recommendations section. A sign of a good candidate is one who is able to link the four quadrants as part of their recommendations. For example, you may suggest a company could utilise a strength to take advantage of an opportunity or to overcome a weakness.

Don't forget that the SWOT exercise which follows next, is based purely on the pre-seen material. To score well for your SWOT in the exam, you must update this with the new issues appearing in the unseen material. If you don't, you will not score marks for your SWOT analysis.

Test your understanding 1 - Basic SWOT

Perform a position audit of D plc using the SWOT analysis model.

Strengths	Weaknesses
Opportunities	**Threats**

Test your understanding 2 - Key issues

Using your SWOT analysis as a starting point pull out the key issues in this case answering the following questions:

(1) What is the issue?

(2) Why is it an issue (i.e. consider implications)?

(3) How should it be resolved (i.e. consider alternative courses of action with justification)?

Issue 1	
Issue 2	
Issue 3	
Issue 4	
Issue 5	
Issue 6	

2 Further reading

In considering the above key issues a number of implementation issues are important:

- How best to reorganise the group, if at all?

- Many of the issues involve change. D plc's culture is likely to be resistant to change so the whole process of how to manage change could be very important

- Should any proposed expansion be facilitated via organic growth or through acquisitions, or even some form of joint venture?

A revision of these concepts is given below.

Organisational structure

Functional structures

A functional structure divides the organisation up into activities or functions (e.g. production, sales, finance, personnel etc.) and places a manager in charge of each function which is then co-ordinated by a narrow band of senior management.

This is a very common form of structure as it allows the deployment of specialisation principles.

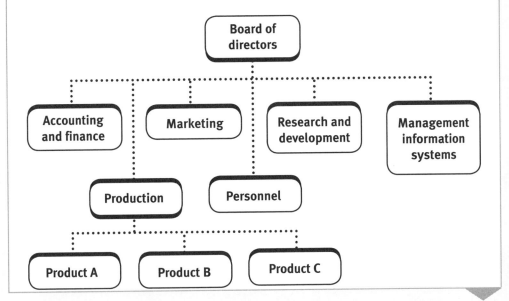

Pros and cons of functional structures

Advantages

- Pooling of expertise, through the grouping of specialised tasks and staff.

- No duplication of functions and economies of scale.

- Senior managers are close to the operation of all functions.

- The facilitation of management and control of functional specialists (suited to centralised organisations).

Disadvantages

- 'Vertical' barriers between functions, that may affect work flow (creating co-ordination problems) and information flow (creating communication problems).

- Focuses on internal processes/inputs rather than outputs such as quality and customer satisfaction through a horizontal value chain.

- Struggles to cope with change, growth and diversification.

- Senior management may not have time to address strategic planning issues.

Divisional structures

Divisional structures empower management teams and subdivide the structure into smaller structures with strategic reporting lines present.

Holding company structures may be apparent and generally the structure divides on the following bases:

- **Product-based structures** divide the organisation along product lines. This is similar to the function ideology except the basis of division will be the market and or product;

- **Geographical structures** divide the structure along the lines of geography i.e. countries or areas and are common in multinational companies.

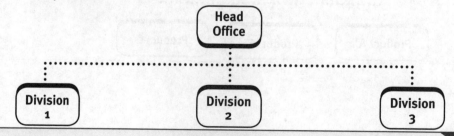

(1)   Product divisions

In a multi-product organisation a product orientation is used as a modification of the functional structure. This structure establishes each product, or group of products, as an integrated unit within the framework of the company. The main functions of production, sales, people and finance are apportioned to the relative products, so that each product group could have its own specialist accounting personnel, technical, etc. Such an organisation allows considerable delegation by top management and clear profit accountability by division heads.

The advantages of product divisionalisation are as follows.

–   The focus of attention is on product performance and profitability. By placing the responsibility for product profitability at the division level, they are able to react and make decisions quickly on a day-to-day basis.

–   It encourages growth and diversity of products, for example, by adding additional flavours, sizes, etc. to capture other segments of the market. This, in turn, promotes the use of specialised equipment, skills and facilities.

–   The role of general manager is encouraged with less concentration upon specialisation. This promotes the wider view of a company's operations – 'the helicopter ability' highly prized by John Harvey-Jones and others.

Product divisionalisation is generally to be preferred over, say, geographic divisionalisation when the product is relatively complex and requires high-cost capital equipment, skilled operators and significant administrative costs. This is the situation in the car industry, farm machinery manufacture and electronics industry.

(2)   Geographical divisions

With geographic divisionalisation, the enterprise is organised by regions or countries. The major international accountancy firms tend to follow this structure. A possible road transport company structure is outlined below:

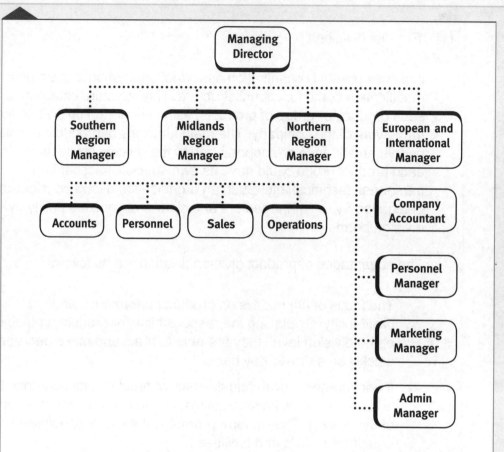

Carried to completion, the geographic division becomes a relatively complete administrative unit in itself. The geographic unit can itself be organised by function or product. The effect of the geographic division at company level is to draw a territorial boundary around these basic components.

Matrix structure

For the larger company the divisional structure is often the most appropriate but it may eventually have to move toward a structure which includes formal mechanisms to promote closer interdivisional collaboration - the result is the **matrix structure** in which dual reporting lines are recognised

e.g. a divisional financial controller has two reporting lines, one to group finance and the other to the divisional management team.

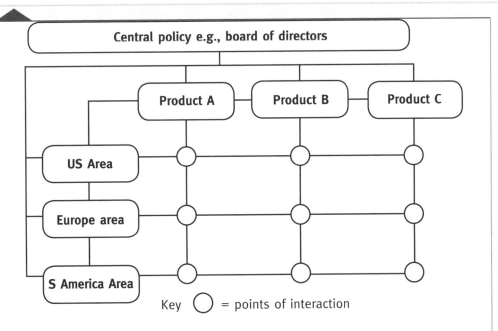

Matrix structures are also widely used for project management.

Pros and cons of matrix structures

Advantages

- organise horizontal groupings of individuals or units into teams that operationally deal with the strategic matter at hand

- are organic with open communications and flexible goals

- may be established as a permanent structure or be temporary to address a particular strategic commitment, such as an export research group to study international markets in a multi-product trading company might establish, or a unique product group for a limited-duration contract

- can creatively serve the needs of strategic change that otherwise might be constrained by more traditional structures

- retain functional economies and product, service or geographical co-ordination

- can improve motivation through:
    - people working participatively in teams
    - specialists broadening their outlook
    - encouraging competition within the organisation.

Disadvantages

- may lead to problems of dual authority with conflict between functional and product or geographical managers leading to individual stress arising from threats to occupational identity, reporting to more than one boss and unclear expectations

- may incur higher administrative costs.

Change Management

Types of change

Change can be classified by the extent of the change required, and the speed with which the change is to be achieved:

		Extent of change	
		Transformation	**Realignment**
Speed of change	**Incremental**	**Evolution:** Transformational change implemented gradually through inter-related initiatives; likely to be proactive change undertaken in participation of the need for future change	**Adaptation:** Change undertaken to realign the way in which the organisation operates; implemented in a series of steps
	Big Bang	**Revolution:** Transformational change that occurs via simultaneous initiatives on many fronts: • more likely to be forced and reactive because of the changing competitive conditions that the organisation is facing	**Reconstruction:** Change undertaken to realign the way in which the organisation operates with many initiatives implemented simultaneously: • often forced and reactive because of a changing competitive context

- Transformation entails changing an organisation's culture. It is a fundamental change that cannot be handled within the existing organisational paradigm.

- Realignment does not involve a fundamental reappraisal of the central assumptions and beliefs.

- Evolution can take a long period of time, but results in a fundamentally different organisation once completed.

- Revolution is likely to be a forced, reactive transformation using simultaneous initiatives on many fronts, and often in a relatively short space of time.

Resistance to change

Resistance may take many forms, including active or passive, overt or covert, individual or organised, aggressive or timid. For each source of resistance, management need to provide an appropriate response, e.g.:

Source of resistance	Possible response
<ul><li>The need for security and the familiar</li><li>Having the opinion that no change is needed</li><li>Poor timing</li><li>Trying to protect vested interests</li></ul>	<ul><li>Provide information and encouragement, invite involvement</li><li>Clarify the purpose of the change and how it will be made</li><li>Demonstrate the problem or the opportunity that makes changes desirable</li></ul>

Managing the change process

The change process – Lewin

The process of change, shown in the diagram below, includes unfreezing habits or standard operating procedures, changing to new patterns and refreezing to ensure lasting effects.

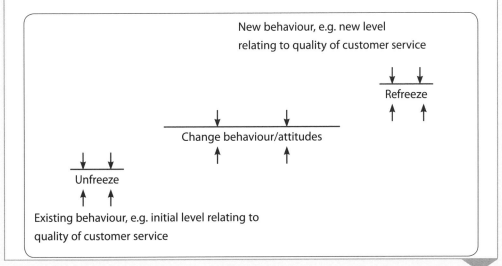

The process of changing the level of quality of customer service comprises three stages.

- Unfreezing – create the initial motivation to change by convincing staff of the undesirability of the present situation.

- The change process itself – mainly concerned with identifying what the new behaviour or norm should be. This stage will often involve new information being communicated and new attitudes, culture and concepts being adopted.

- Refreezing or stabilising the change – implying reinforcement of the new pattern of work or behaviour by rewards (praise, etc).

Force field analysis

Lewin also emphasised the importance of force field analysis. He argued that managers should consider any change situation in terms of:

- the factors encouraging and facilitating the change (the driving forces)

- the factors that hinder change (the restraining forces).

If we want to bring about change we must disturb the equilibrium by:

- strengthening the driving forces

- weakening the restraining forces

- or both.

The model encourages us to identify the various forces impinging on the target of change, to consider the relative strengths of these forces and to explore alternative strategies for modifying the force field.

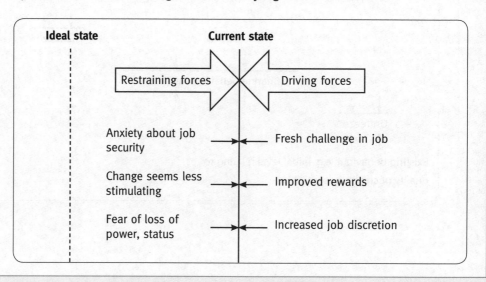

Methods of expansion

Acquisition v organic growth

Organic growth is internally generated growth within the firm.

Growth strategy

Assuming a standard profit maximising company, the primary purpose of any growth strategy should be to increase shareholder wealth.

- No external growth should be considered unless the organic alternative has been dismissed as inferior.

Advantages of acquisitions over organic growth

Acquisition has some significant advantages over internal growth.

- High-speed access to resources – this is particularly true of brands; an acquisition can provide a powerful brand name that could take years to establish through internal growth.

- Avoids barriers to entry – acquisition may be the only way to enter a market where the competitive structure would not admit a new member or the barriers to entry were too high.

- Less reaction from competitors – there is less likelihood of retaliation because an acquisition does not alter the capacity of the competitive arena.

- It can block a competitor – if Kingfisher's bid for Asda had been successful it would have denied Walmart its easy access to the UK.

- It can help restructure the operating environment – some mergers of car companies were used to reduce overcapacity.

- Relative price/earnings ratio – if the P/E ratio is significantly higher in the new industry than the present one, acquisition may not be possible because it would cause a dilution in earnings per share to the existing shareholders. But if the present company has a high P/E ratio it can boost earnings per share by issuing its own equity in settlement of the purchase price.

- Asset valuation – if the acquiring company believes the potential acquisition's assets are undervalued, it might undertake an asset-stripping operation.

Disadvantages of acquisitions growth

There are some disadvantages associated with this method of growth.

- Acquisition may be more costly than internal growth because the owners of the acquired company will have to be paid for the risk already taken. On the other hand, if the company decides on internal growth, it will have to bear the costs of the risk itself.

- There is bound to be a cultural mismatch between the organisations – a lack of 'fit' can be significant in knowledge-based companies, where the value of the business resides in individuals.

- Differences in managers' salaries – another example of cultural mismatch that illustrates how managers are valued in different countries.

- Disposal of assets – companies may be forced to dispose of assets they had before the acquisition. The alliance between British Airways and American Airlines was called off because the pair would have had to free up around 224 take-off and landing slots to other operators.

- Risk – of not knowing all there is to know about the business it seeks to buy.

- Reduction in return on capital employed – quite often an acquisition adds to sales and profit volume without adding to value creation.

Other reasons for acquisitions

Whilst the potential for synergy is a key reason given for growth by acquisitions other motives do exist:

- Entry to new markets and industries.

- To acquire the target company's staff and know-how.

- Managerial motives – conscious pursuit of self-interest by managers.

- Arrogance factor/Hubris hypothesis.

- Diversification.

- A defence mechanism to prevent being taken over.

- A means of improving liquidity.

- Improved ability to raise finance.

- A reduction of risk by acquiring substantial assets (if the predator has a high earnings to net asset ratio and is in a risky business).

- To obtain a growth company (especially if the predator's growth is declining).

- To create a situation where rationalisation (which would otherwise be shirked) may be carried out more acceptably.

Joint methods of expansion

With any joint arrangement key issues will relate to:

- sharing out risks and returns
- funding
- decision making
- ownership, especially of intellectual property
- scope, including geographical and possibly timescales

Joint ventures

A separate business entity whose shares are owned by two or more business entities. Assets are formally integrated and jointly owned.

The advantages of using a company as the vehicle for expansion are that:

- a company is a universally recognised medium and gives a strong identity for dealings with third parties;
- it allows for a management and employee structure to be put in place;
- the participants have the benefit of a limited liability and the flexibility to raise finance; and
- the company will survive as the same entity despite a change in its share ownership;

Key issues in setting up a joint venture include considering the following:

Shareholders' agreement

- The purpose of a shareholders' agreement will be to establish the basic rights and obligations of the parties and to ensure the company and its business are established and run in accordance with the participants' objectives.
- A further purpose is to prescribe, as far as possible, for what will happen if difficulties occur.

The Board of Directors

- Directors will be appointed by both joint venture participants.

- An individual director may face a conflict between the interests of the venture and interests of his appointing company.

- To the extent that there are areas for conflict, it may be better for these to be dealt with at shareholder level rather than Board level.

Dealing with deadlock

- Deadlock can arise either in a 50/50 joint venture where the shareholders' appointed directors take opposing views or where a director appointed by a minority shareholder exercises the right to veto.

- Similarly, deadlock can arise at shareholder level in relation to matters which require shareholder approval.

- Options for dealing with deadlock include giving the chairman the casting vote, referral to an independent third party (for example, a non-executive director) or referring directly back to the shareholders.

- Provision must also be made for if an insoluble deadlock arises. In such cases recommendations could involve liquidation, the transfer of shares to a third party or a "russian roulette clause" that allows one party to sell their shares to the other at a predetermined price. In the latter case, the other party can either accept the offer or reverse it at the same price. This risk of reversal acts as an incentive to the offering party to put forward a fair price.

Funding

- The parties must agree how much capital and in what form each party will contribute and arrangements for ongoing funding should the need arise.

Transfer of shares

- The parties entering into a joint venture do not normally expect the other party to dispose of its shareholding to a third party since the result could well be that two incompatible parties are thrown together.

- It is therefore common for joint ventures to restrict the transfer of shares without consent of the other party or for the other party to have first refusal ('pre-emption rights')

Intellectual property

- Particularly important in the event of a transfer of a party's shares or early termination of the venture is the need to establish what happens to the technology and other intellectual property rights of the joint venture company.

Test your understanding answers

Test your understanding 1 - Basic SWOT

Strengths	Weaknesses

• Strong financials - improving revenue, operating margins and net profit, despite difficult economic conditions.
 	
 • Board have successfully cut operating costs to boost profits.
 	
 • Listed company so should find it easier to raise funds.
 	
 • Brands strategy allows greater focus on particular segments.
	• Board seem reluctant to change anything and lack ambition.
	
	 • Formal and inflexible planning process
	
	 • Lack of investment in MMC.
	
	 • Complex organisational structure
	    – Lack of integration of IT systems from acquired companies
	    – Duplication of effort
	    – Rivalry and conflict between divisional managers
	
	 • Failure to manage acquired businesses adequately.
	
	 • Poor staff training (NN).
	
	 • Poor sourcing of supplies (NN).

Opportunities	Threats
• Reorganise to gain greater cost efficiencies and standardisation • Reduce direct costs as stated • Government policies on the use of greenfield v brownfield sites and any assistance given to help with the latter. • Increased demand for new houses across the full range of sizes and styles as a result of demographic change (people living longer, divorce rates etc) • Expansion into building commercial property such as offices and factories • Convergence of tastes will create opportunities (e.g. expansion into Country Y) • Other overseas expansion • Further acquisitions of rivals as some may be suffering in the recession • Backward vertical integration to acquire a firm that manufactures / develops MMC. products.	• High competitive rivalry within the UK (note: we are told that at least one competitor has performed better than D plc in the recession) • If rivals gain local expertise and knowledge in D plc's main markets, then its core competences, and hence competitive advantage, could be undermined • Recession in the UK means there are few growth opportunities • If interest rates go up, then demand for housing will deteriorate further. • The credit crisis still means that it is harder to borrow funds - this affects both the building companies and their ultimate customers • Lack of confidence in the UK buy-to-let market • Government plans for zero-carbon houses by 2016 (you could have argued that this is an opportunity or a threat, depending on how D plc responds to it!) • Localism Act in UK - gives more power to local communities to influence planning decisions

Test your understanding 2 - Key issues

Issue 1	Market stagnation (threat)
	The main problem facing D plc is the market stagnation in the UK. This is due to the following

- Economic recession that may have years to run before growth returns
- Fears over unemployment and the possibility of interest rate rises make first time buyers less confident
- Once they have decided to buy a house, many people are still finding problems getting mortgages. Despite steps such as quantitative easing, there is still a credit crunch.
- A lack of confidence in the buy to let market

The main implication of this is that there are very few opportunities for growth over the next few years if D plc continues with its current strategy. This is a key problem because D plc is listed and larger shareholders are unlikely to be satisfied with such an outlook. This could result in the following

- A fall in share price
- Problem raising further funds
- Unless the board can come up with alternative plans, then they may see their roles terminated.

Possible courses of action include the following:

- Reposition the group to take advantage of the opportunities that do exist within the UK market - e.g. greater use of MMC, drive towards making more energy-efficient houses
- Consider expansion into new markets, such as Country Y

Issue 2	**The Board of Directors (weakness)**
	The Board of Directors is a major weakness of D plc. This is illustrated by the following: • Lack of Board responsiveness to market trends - e.g. unwillingness to invest in MMC • The board do not seem concerned that a competitor has performed better in the recession than D plc - e.g. The CEO and Chairman see no reason to change the way they do business • Over-formal rigid planning process - e.g. strategy only really reviewed once a year • Inability to see the bigger picture - e.g. see this recession as simply part of the business cycle • The only plan the Board has devised is further cost cutting • Lacked the commitment to rationalise the systems of newly acquired businesses • The NED NN has suggested problems with IT and training but has not been listened to. The main implication of this is that D plc will fail to address the threats to its business (e.g. erosion of its core competences due to new entrants) and will fail to exploit its opportunities (e.g. use of MMC). As stated above it is likely that shareholders will be disatisfied with this performance, especially taking together the weak Board, no dividend, no growth prospects and falling behind a rival. To redeem the operation of the Board the following steps could be taken: • Adopt a more responsive, even emergent approach to strategy. • Complete a full strategic review. This needs to be actioned and acted upon quickly to reassure shareholders • Switch to meeting every month • Consider the strengths or weaknesses of each Director with a view to replacing some with more dynamic proactive people.

Issue 3	**Problematic group structure (weakness)**
	The current group structure is overly complex with effectively 9 business units with a lack of effective integration and coordination. This is illustrated by the following: • Rivalry and conflict between managers, especially when a development overlaps two different regions • Lack of integration and standardisation of IT systems • Duplication of effort in marketing and sales and operations and procurement The main implication of this is that the structure erodes D plc's competitive advantage: • Procurement costs are higher than they need to be with nine procurement functions rather than one centralised one • Brand strength and the marketing effort will be undermined by a lack of standardisation - e.g. within the S brand there are three different managers responsible for marketing • Quality and costs could be undermined by not having consistent staff training (an issue raised by NN) • Higher costs due to duplication of effort The obvious step that could be taken is to restructure the group. Possible courses of action include: • Centralise the IT, HR and finance functions to head office. There is little advantage operating these on a divisional basis and centralisation should result in better integration and cost savings. • Adopt a matrix structure with heads of **regions** and heads of **function**. This will ensure – A local regional emphasis is continued (contribution to D plc's core competences) – Better standardisation within functions - e.g. having a national approach to marketing – The potential problem is that brand management may suffer - e.g. lack of standardised designs across all H houses.

	• Adopt a matrix structure with heads of **regions** and heads of **brand/product**. This will ensure 　– A local emphasis is continued (contribution to D plc's core competences) 　– Better brand management - e.g. standardised designs across all H houses 　– The potential problem is that the authority of functional heads is diluted resulting in inconsistent marketing, for example. • Adopt a three way matrix with heads of region, function and brand to get all the above benefits. Ultimately the decision comes down to which perspectives are most important - local emphasis v brand v function.
Issue 4	**Market trends (opportunity)** Despite the overall recession, there are significant opportunities in the UK market. In particular: • Increasing demand for energy-efficient housing • Greater regulation - developments in MMC The implications of these depends on how D plc responds. If D plc continues as it is, then: • its competitive advantage will continue to be eroded, • it will continue to struggle for growth, • it won't be ready to meet future regulations (e.g. carbon neutral housing by 2016), • its reputation will be undermined by a lack of green credentials, • all of which will make it more difficult for D plc to gain planning permission and acquire land for larger developments and • it will result in lower demand for D plc houses

	The alternative is to take action immediately:
	• D plc is lagging behind rivals so trying to develop in-house expertise in MMC will take too long to address the problem. Instead expertise could be acquired in some way.
	• One approach would be to source suppliers with the required expertise. The problem here is that this then effectively becomes a threshold competence rather than a core competence as rivals will be able to use the same supplier.
	• An alternative would be to look to buy a supplier with the skills and expertise needed.
	• A third market solution would be to buy a patent covering the expertise and technology needed.
Issue 5	**The role of Government (could be opportunity or threat)** Acquiring land in the right place at the right price and getting planning permission are critical success factors in the industry. Both of these are heavily influenced by Government, for example: • Local government planning offices have the power to grant or refuse permission • The Localism Act has given more power to local communities to block planning permission • Government plans for zero-carbon houses by 2016 • Government policies on the use of greenfield v brownfield sites and any assistance given to help with the latter. • Government intervention in the financial sector to try to boost liquidity and lending (e.g quantitative easing)

	It is vital that D plc is aware of Government plans and responds to them to avoid decline. In particular D plc could consider the following:
	
	• Developing its relationship with government
	   – Lobbying parliament to change restrictive legislation (e.g. on the use of Greenbelt land)
	   – Employ researchers to determine and analyse government plans more efficiently
	
	• Be more responsive to government plans
	   – Develop expertise in the adoption of brownfield sites - e.g. dealing with toxic chemicals
	   – Adoption of MMC to improve energy efficiency

Issue 6	**Expansion into Country Y (opportunity)** The possibility of expansion into Country Y needs to be taken seriously for two reasons: • There are limited growth opportunities for D plc within the UK and institutional shareholders may demand more ambitious plans from the Board. • The examiner rarely includes this much text on a possible opportunity in the preseen information without testing it in at least one of the real exams based on that case! Advantages of investing in Y include the following: • rapid growth • increasing demand for UK-style housing and the skills and expertise needed to build them. D plc may have a competitive advantage here over domestic rivals.

Disadvantages and potential problems include the following:

- the need to acquire the CSF of local knowledge

- political instability, including militant groups with "simmering resentment"

- risk of earthquakes and typhoons will influnce designs. This is not an area of expertise D plc currently has!

- differences in governance and social responsibility will either mean D plc has higher costs than local rivals (if it maintains current high standards) or exposes it to reputational risk back in the UK if it adopts local standards.

- similarly local corruption could make it difficult for D plc to compete without adopting similar practices.

- The family ownership structure of domestic firms and a culture of ignoring other stakeholder interests may make joint ventures difficult to manage.

Other considerations

- Given the Sales Director's contacts in country Y, there is definitely scope for "dubious" buisness practices, especially if the Sales Director is involved in making any decisions regarding the venture. To what extent are his views designed to maximise D plc's shareholder wealth or are they to benefit friends, family and himself?

- If D plc decides to invest in Country Y, then which approach should be adopted - organic growth, acquisition or joint venture?

Prioritising issues

Chapter learning objectives

By the end of this chapter you will:

- Have practised the prioritisation processes to prioritise sets of issues relevant to the current case

- Have seen a broad range of potential issues which may arise in your actual exam

1 The importance of selecting the right issues

The assessment criterion of prioritisation is worth a maximum of 5 marks to your overall score. It might therefore seem surprising that we are devoting a full chapter to the subject!

It is important to recognise that prioritisation marks are specifically awarded for the ordering of your issues and more importantly, the justification you provide of that ordering. The overall process of selecting which four issues you will discuss and in which order is however worth significantly more as it will impact on your judgement and logic marks, which, in respect of requirement 1(a), account for a total of 40 marks.

It is therefore not surprising that this initial stage of the exam process; the reading of the material and the decision over which issues to cover, is the one where many students have the most problems.

This chapter will give some additional guidance, specific to the current case, to help you improve in this area.

2 Using your 20 minutes reading time effectively

The issue selection and prioritisation process must begin as soon as you start reading the un-seen information. Every second counts within the case study exam and so it's important to use all of your time effectively.

Within the 20 minutes reading time you are only allowed to annotate the exam paper. You cannot use any other paper or start typing on your computer. As a result, any process you adopt must be concise whilst still allowing you to capture all of your thoughts.

Furthermore, the process must suit you! Everyone is different and what might work for one person could be a disaster for another. For example, some people prefer to work with lists, other with mindmaps. Practise different techniques to find a method you prefer and that works for you.

At the end of the process (which may take longer than the 20 minutes reading time), you should aim to have:

- Identified which four issues you will discuss in the main body of your report

- Assigned a loose prioritisation to the issues (the final order might not be clear until after you have performed some calculations)

- Prepared some brief notes / thoughts on alternative solutions (together with pros and cons)

- Decided on the five technical models and five diversity comments you will include in your report (including a note of where you intend to use them)

- Considered any linkages between the issues presented in the un-seen
- Identified two ethical issues to discuss

Some additional guidance

(1) Regardless of which process you end up adopting, it is recommended that you start your planning on the reverse of the detachable page within the exam paper. In most cases, this will give you a virtually blank piece of paper on which to work your magic!

(2) Never attack your exam paper with a chunky highlighter. The problem with highlighters is you can end up highlighting virtually everything (particularly in the case study exam when most information provided in the un-seen will be relevant) and are unable to write down any of the thoughts you have as you perform your initial read. Instead, use a normal pen and make notes in the margin of the exam paper. If you want to underline something specific, ensure you note why you thought it needed underlining. For example, you might underline a figure because you will need it to perform a calculation or you might underline a date because it indicates an urgent deadline.

(3) You should always read the requirement first to ensure you identify any specific requirements. For example, are you told of an aspect that you must include in your report or is your report to be directed at a specific director or group of directors.

(4) Read about each bold heading in turn and be clear about both the event and the underlying issue. You must focus your discussions on the issue.

3 Suggested Prioritisation Processes

In Kaplan's Case Study Skills Development text, we highlighted three suggested processes that experience has shown, often works for students in the exam. That isn't to say that these are the only methods, just the most common. Remember, you will need to find a way that suits you. Given below is a quick reminder of those techniques.

The ordered list

This process is ideally suited to people who prefer lists and structure.

Step 1: Begin by reading everything under the first bold heading. Make notes in the margins concerning the impact, urgency and size of the issue. Also jot down any ideas on alternative solutions. Ensure you have identified the issue and then write this in the middle of your planning sheet (use the detachable page from the exam paper)
If you think the issue also has an ethical dimension, put a star next to it.

Step 2:   Read everything under the second bold heading, making notes as you did in step 1.

To add this issue to your planning sheet, you must consider whether it should be prioritised above or below the first issue. To decide you will need to quickly review your notes about urgency, size and most importantly the impact of the issue on the strategic objectives of the business.

Add this issue to your planning sheet, either above or below the first issue depending on what you decide.

Ensure you note down your reasoning (this can be used to help write up your prioritisation section later)

Step 3:   Repeat step 2 for all of the remaining bold headings on the exam paper.

Step 4:   Review your list to identify any linkages. Can two issues be condensed into one because they are very similar? Could you use one issue as a potential solution for another? Will one issue impact on the recommendations you can provide on another?

Mark the linkages on your planning sheet

Step 5:   Now, for your top four issues, consider which technical models and diversity comments you will be able to use. Note these down on the right hand side of your planning sheet against the issue where you plan to include it.

You may also want to include a model or real world comment in your introduction. Note these at the top of your sheet.

The extended mindmap

This process is ideally suited to those who prefer pictures and diagrams to trigger their thoughts.

Step 1:   Read the un-seen information making notes in the margins concerning the impact, urgency and size of each issue. Also jot down any ideas on alternative solutions.

As you read convert each event into an issue and then write the issue in a "bubble" on your planning sheet (use the detachable page from the exam paper)

If you think the issue also has an ethical dimension, put a star next to it.

Step 2:   Keep adding each new issue you identify to your sheet. At the end you should have a page with a number of bubbles dotted about.

Step 3: Review your bubbles to identify any linkages. Can two issues be condensed into one because they are very similar? Could you use one issue as a potential solution for another? Will one issue impact on the recommendations you can provide on another?

Mark the linkages on your planning sheet by connecting the bubbles.

Step 4: Review your notes about urgency, size and most importantly the impact of the issue on the strategic objectives of the business. Use these to decide on the order in which you should cover the issues. Place numbers next to your bubbles to indicate your decision, ensuring that you keep a note of your reasoning to help when you come to write up your prioritisation section.

Step 5: Now, for your top four issues, consider which technical models and diversity comments you will be able to use. Note these down above each bubble where you plan to use the model.

You may also want to include a model or real world comment in your introduction. Note these at the top of your sheet.

Ranking using your SWOT

This process will help those who find it difficult to make the prioritisation decision.

Step 1: On your planning sheet (use the detachable page from the exam paper), set out headings from strengths, weaknesses etc.

As you read the un-seen information making notes in the margins concerning the impact, urgency and size of each issue. Also jot down any ideas on alternative solutions. Convert each event into an issue and then write the issue on your planning sheet under the appropriate heading.

If you think the issue also has an ethical dimension, put a star next to it.

Step 2: Keep adding each new issue you identify to your sheet. At the end you should have a virtually complete SWOT.

Step 3: Review your SWOT to identify any linkages. Can two issues be condensed into one because they are very similar? Could you use one issue as a potential solution for another? Will one issue impact on the recommendations you can provide on another?

Mark the linkages on your planning sheet.

Step 4: Review your notes about urgency, likelihood and most importantly the impact of the issue on the strategic objectives of the business. Assign a score out of 10 (10 being high) for each of these three criteria. Use the total to decide on the order in which you should cover the issues. Place numbers next to each issue to indicate your decision.

Step 5: Now, for your top four issues, consider which technical models and diversity comments you will be able to use. Note these down on your planning sheet making sure you also write which section of your report you intend to include it in.

Note: After completing your prioritisation process, you may want to add a couple of additional items to your SWOT based on the pre-seen material. This will ensure you SWOT has sufficient depth and balance. Choose issues from the pre-seen that support the new issues you've been presented within the exam.

Whilst these processes do have similarities, they also have subtle differences that bring about advantages and disadvantages.

Process one places the emphasis on the prioritisation decision whereas process two emphasises the identification of linkages between issues. Process three can help the prioritisation process but can feel rather robotic and can result in an ordering that might not reflect true commercial reality. Unfortunately in the case study exam, not everything fits into a nice little box!

The following test your understandings will allow you to practise each of the processes using relatively simplistic scenarios. This will help you to gain a better understanding of what works for you.

Prioritisation exercise 1

You are told of the following events in the un-seen information:

- In recent years the UK has enjoyed an influx of skilled tradesmen from European countries, in particular Eastern Europe. D plc has been able to take advantage of this large supply of relatively cheap but skilled labour. Many of these tradesmen have been in the UK for several years now and a significant proportion are now choosing to move back to their home countries

  As such the company is currently experiencing a shortage of skilled and qualified electricians across the whole of the Eastern region. The Operations Manager of the region is particularly concerned that this is the start of a long term shortage and worries about the impact this will have on the cost of such skilled labour. This shortage of workers is affecting the company's ability to complete several developments in the area.

- Since the release of the 2011 accounts for D plc, there has been a series of board room disputes.

  The Sales Director, who was already disillusioned at the lack of growth in the forecast over the next three years, was the most vocal board member and felt that D had not been robust enough in both financial and strategic planning.

  The Sales Director handed in his resignation last week; his contract requires him to provide 3 month's notice period. He is leaving to go to a competitor, who has also offered him a comparable salary, and has just announced an aggressive overseas expansion strategy.

- The General Manager of the Northern Region recently met with a newspaper reporter from a local free newspaper. The reporter explained that he intended to run a story next week alleging that toxic material cleared from a Brownfield site, currently being developed by H, was dumped in a public landfill site without permission.

  The initial site clearance contract of the Brownfield site, including the removal of the toxic material, was sub-contracted to X Ltd – a small local site clearance specialist. The full cost of cleaning the land fill site, including proper disposal of the toxic material will cost £100,000.

- The Northern Region General Manager has asked for your assistance in assessing the potential of a piece of 'brownfield' land that the division is considering purchasing.

  The land will cost £16 million. As an existing brownfield site, the manager is confident that planning permission will be granted for a development of 200 homes, provided a quantity of low-cost affordable housing is included alongside the more premium homes.

  Although some initial discussions with the planning authorities have taken place, there are still a number of uncertainties regarding the exact mix of housing, general house price movements in the area and the cost of construction. The development team have produced a number of forecasts with associated probabilities for you to evaluate.

  In order for sufficient access to the development to be secured, D plc would also have to buy an adjacent strip of land currently owned by Mrs Grey. A valuer appointed by D plc has estimated that the fair value of the land, given the proposed use, is £400,000. Without the development, the value of the land is approximately £50,000. Mrs Grey is unaware of the value of the land she owns.

- D plc has a whistleblowing telephone line where employees can leave a confidential message if they have concerns with the ethical behaviour of a colleague or the ethical activities of the company as a whole.

  The HR director has been passed a recorded message that implies that the planning team in the Northern region have been making facilitation payments to local authority managers in order to speed up the planning process. An initial investigation so far has identified no unauthorised, inappropriate or unethical payments.

Required:

Prepare the prioritisation section of your report.

Prioritisation exercise 2

You are told of the following events in the un-seen information:

- D currently uses local suppliers for raw materials such as wood, concrete and bricks. Within each regional division, the local procurement manager sources the supplier and agrees at current market rates for prices.

  Following on from a procurement managers' meeting in the central region, a proposal has emerged. A national supplier of bricks – GreatBricks – had contacted the regional manager and suggested a deal to supply all the bricks for every D house nationwide. They have offered a range of options to D for the length of contract signed, ranging from one to five years.

- An article in the property section of a regional weekend paper has recently highlighted some confusion regarding D's portfolio. One example of this concerns a four-bedroomed house design with an integral garage. This is a very popular design used on many of D's developments across the country. It is used on both H and R developments although it is called The Monarch design by H and The Prince by R.

  A property journalist, recognising that these two houses were both built to exactly the same design and specification, has done some price comparisons and identified that the design is currently being marketed by the two different businesses at significantly different prices. Although much of this can be attributed to differing land values, there are some examples of situations where properties on neighbouring sites are marketed at different prices.

This has highlighted to D plc that internally and externally there is some confusion regarding the different brands. The CEO of D plc believes this is due to the fact that marketing activity is carried out at central, regional and business level and believes the best way to solve the problem is through a company restructure.

- At a recent D plc Board meeting, the CEO highlighted a potential opportunity to the Board. A close friend of the CEO is the Managing Director (MD) of F Ltd, a house-builder based in Devon in the South-West of England has asked if D plc may be interested in buying the company. D plc does not currently have any significant operations in the region.

  In 2012, F Ltd took on a major development not far from Plymouth on a site located within an existing flood plain. Whilst all precautions were taken, the site was subject to flooding during the recent freak rain storms leaving the company with significant clean-up costs. In addition to this development, the only other development F Ltd has in the pipeline relates to strategic land in owns with a current book value of £40 million. However, it is thought highly likely that planning permission will be granted on this land, meaning its fair value will increase to an estimated £50 million. F Ltd was planning on developing this land throughout 2013 - 2015, building an estimated 650 homes. This land is regarded as premium and is not located in a flood plain.

  In addition to the above land, F Ltd is forecast to have non-current assets of £0.5m and inventory of £2 million, all of which will relate to construction work in progress on the affected site. The company has debt finance with a book value of £35m, an is expected to have an overdraft of £3 million and trade payables of £0.3m. F Ltd's MD has also supplied forecast income statements covering 2013 to 2015.

  The MD of F Ltd has also approached another national house-builder, in addition to D plc in order to gauge their interest. He has stated however, that he believes D plc offers a better match for the business.

- The Standard Assessment Procedure (SAP) is the UK Department of Energy and Climate Change's methodology for assessing and comparing the energy and environmental performance of homes. Its purpose is to provide accurate and reliable assessments of home energy performances in order to provide the information needed to develop appropriate energy and environmental policy initiatives.

SAP works by assessing how much energy a home will consume and how much carbon dioxide will be emitted in delivering a defined level of temperature and living conditions. These assessments enable a like for like comparison of home carbon emissions and energy efficiency, with each home being given a rating between 1 (poor) and 100 (good).

It has been proposed that from 2013 new legislation will require all new houses to achieve a minimum SAP rating of 80. However, this is still to be approved by Parliament and some critics are suggesting it is unlikely that this proposal will be enacted.

D's average SAP rating is currently 73. Although the properties built by H and R are marginally above the required standard, the overall rating is being pulled down by houses built under the S brand.

- The General Manager of the Eastern Region has recently received a complaint letter from a lady regarding a recent visit she made to view a show home on one of D plc's mixed housing developments. Whilst in the show home, the lady fell and damaged her hip. She is alleging that she tripped on a trailing computer cable that wasn't adequately protected.

  She has advised that she will be contacting an 'accident claims' bureau in order to make a claim against the company.

Required:

Prepare the prioritisation section of your report.

Test your understanding answers

Prioritisation exercise 1

3 Prioritisation of issues

The following issues have been prioritised from the SWOT analysis in Appendix A:

3.1 Resignation of Sales Director

The top priority is to address the resignation of the sales director. This is a corporate governance issue and as D is a listed company the impact of the resignation on shareholder confidence must be effectively managed. It could also impact the strategic growth of D plc as the knowledge and contacts of the sales director within Country Y could impact the company's ability to expand into this market. There is a risk that the opportunity will be exploited by the competitor the sales director intends to join.

The company must initially decide whether to try and retain the services of the sales director and if not make arrangements for their replacement and how best to communicate the news to the market.

3.2 Labour shortage

The second priority is to address the labour shortage in the Eastern region both from a short term and long term perspective. The shortage is damaging the ability of the company to deliver operational results and will increase costs that will damage the financial performance of the business if solutions are not urgently identified and implemented.

As the shortage is currently only impacting one region is it prioritised below the sales director resignation. The board need to agree short term measures to alleviate the current problem and implement longer term solutions to protect the future labour supply.

3.3 Land acquisition

The third priority is to assess the proposed £16m acquisition of the brownfield site in the Northern region. The purchase would add to the company's strategic land bank and help it to deliver future financial targets.

This type of proposal assessment, whilst important and relatively urgent, is really 'business as usual' for D plc and therefore it has been ranked below the top two issues. The board need to decide whether or not to proceed with the acquisition and decide an initial offer price for the land. There is also an ethical issue to be considered relating to the price to be offered to Mrs Grey for the 'access strip' of land.

3.4 Bad press

The fourth priority is the potential newspaper report alleging toxic material has been dumped in a public landfill. Publication of this story could damage the reputation of D plc and ultimately could impact its perception by customers and shareholders. However as this story has not yet been printed and is only known at a local level the level of reputational damage that could be caused is estimated to be low. Additionally the relatively small cleanup cost and fact that the clearance contract was sub-contracted makes this issue less of a priority.

3.5 Other issues

The allegation of facilitation payments appears to have no foundation and without any tangible evidence means that it is ranked below the above issues.

Prioritisation exercise 2

Section 3 Prioritisation Statement

The following issues have been identified from the SWOT analysis in Appendix A.

3.1 Acquisition of F

The most important issue facing D is the need to make a decision regarding the possible acquisition of F. The acquisition could provide an opportunity for D to deliver much needed revenue growth over the next few years. If D delay a decision regarding the acquisition it is possible that a competitor could enter negotiations with F instead and D could lose out on a valuable opportunity.

The Board need to take care over this decision given the problems F is experiencing with its current development.

This is considered the most important issue due to the urgency of a response and the significant growth potential this acquisition would allow in a new region of the UK.

3.2 Confusion regarding D's portfolio

The second most important issue facing D is the need to ensure a more consistent approach to branding. If this is not resolved, sales in all of D's business could be adversely affected and could result in the company owning housing stock which it is unable to sell.

A decision regarding the structure of the organisation needs to be made as soon as possible in order that steps can be taken to implement the proposals and minimise any potential conflicts arising.

However, this has been assessed of lesser importance than the acquisition since the issue has only been reported in a regional paper and so is unlikely, at this time, to result in much immediate reputational damage.

3.3 Long term supply contract

The next issue which D needs to consider is the proposal to enter into a long term supply agreement with GreatBricks. This proposal has the potential to reduce costs in all divisions of the company and this could have a much needed positive impact on the overall margin of D plc.

The Board needs to ensure the cost savings are not outweighed by logistical delays or reductions in quality; this is of concern given that D plc have never dealt with GreatBricks before.

It is unlikely that GreatBricks need an immediate decision and therefore this issue is considered less urgent than the previous two.

3.4 New legislation

The final issue which affects D is the new legislation which is planned affecting the energy efficiency of new homes built. Implementing changes which will reduce the carbon emissions will allow D to continue to promote the quality of their developments.

However this potential change is not considered as urgent as the previous issues as there is no certainty that the legislation will be enacted. Equally, it would only affect one of D plc's brands so does not have the same reach across the company.

3.5 Other issues

The issue relating to the accident on one of the developments will be considered in the ethical section of this report as will the potential conflict of interest between the Chief Executive of D and the Managing Director of F.

Planning your answer: Mini-case scenarios

Chapter learning objectives

By the end of this chapter you will:

- Be aware of a number of different thinking techniques that can be used to help generate ideas in the exam.

- Understand the different types of issues that each process is best used for.

- Have practiced these techniques when planning and writing answers for a number of different issue types.

1 The importance of judgement and logic marks

Together, judgement and logic marks account for 40 of the 90 marks available for requirement 1(a). So, it's no surprise that there is a strong correlation between those students who score well within these two criteria and those that ultimately pass the exam.

Unfortunately, to earn marks within these criteria you have to demonstrate a set of skills that aren't easily learned from a text book; it's not as simple as memorising a technical model and regurgitating it in the exam. As a result, these are often the two criteria where students score the lowest marks.

To score well you need to plan your answer by analysing a situation, thinking through the implications (including the results of your financial analysis), identifying possible courses of action and evaluating each in the context of a business environment in order to deliver justified, practical recommendations. The most common blockage to this process is in generating the ideas, and that's where a system or technique, designed to structure and stimulate your thoughts, can be very useful.

2 Issue types

Broadly speaking issues can be classified as either *problems* or *opportunities*.

A **problem** issue is best tackled by considering the impact and then identifying and evaluating alternative solutions.   The sort of issues we see arising as problems within the exam include:

- **A corporate governance issue**: For example, a senior director or crucial staff member might be leaving or could be "distracted" from their job. This sort of issue will raise questions over stakeholder confidence, and can lead to concerns with both short and long term operations.

- **A threat to competitive advantage**: An issue of this type is all about the core and threshold competencies and the idea of the "slip". You will be dealing with an issue that threatens the means by which the company achieves success and as such is it will usually be a high priority. Your analysis will need to focus on the impact of the issue and how the company can limit any damage.

- **A threat to the ability to deliver results**: This is quite a common issue where the company concerned is a plc. For example, the company has a published five year plan that it is not meeting due to market pressures. It is often linked with a threat to competitive advantage. This will be a significant issue for shareholders and you will be expected to consider ways in which performance could be improved. This sort of issue can be presented in two different ways. In some scenarios, you are given a range of potential solutions to analyse. In others you will be given more of a "free rein" to suggest potential solutions.

- **A threat to the future survival of the business**: If such an issue arises, it will always be a high priority. In a recent post-exam guidance issued by the examiner, it stated "The most crucial of all issues affecting a company is maintaining its very existence". Such an issue will require detailed advice on how to resolve the situation. The sort of issue that comes under this heading would be a take over of the company or something that threatens going concern.

To cover an **opportunity** you will need to assess the logic of the proposal before identifying the advantages and disadvantages to the company. The sort of issues we see arising as opportunities within the exam include:

- **A strategic proposal**: The majority of proposals presented in the exam will need to be evaluated. You will need to consider both the advantages and disadvantages as well as thinking about the availability of resources and questioning the strategic logic of any potential project.

- **The implementation of an agreed strategy**: Depending on the specifics of the company and the strategy, this can either be a problem or an opportunity. As an agreed strategy, the issue is often more about managing the change process. Such an issue is usually given a lower priority.

- **An event that alters business strategy**: Again, this can either be a problem or an opportunity. For example, the company could face a problem if a new competitor entered the market or could have an opportunity if new legislation opened up new markets. Either way, its business strategy will need to change. You will be expected to analyse the potential changes that could be made.

3 Technical models and diversity points

Whilst thinking in terms of problems and opportunities may provide you with some useful sub-headings for your report, it does not necessarily help to drive your thoughts and ideas.

Perhaps one of the best techniques for generating ideas is to use the various technical models to help analyse the information or to reveal potential courses of action. Equally, examples of real life companies that have been in similar situations is a great prompt for identifying the impact of an issue or actions to be taken.

Both of these methods have the added advantage of picking up marks under other criteria (technical, application and diversity) in addition to just judgement and logic.

To use this technique properly though, you must think about these at the beginning of the planning phase, not at the end. It's no good getting to the end of your plan before thinking 'what technical models can I squeeze into my answer?' Your technical models should drive your thoughts, not tag on at the end.

However, in some situations you might struggle to think of a suitable technical model, or a decent example from the real world. It's in these cases that you need another suite of techniques up your sleeve.

4 Thinking techniques

Thinking techniques force you to consider different perspectives allowing you to access a greater range of ideas and add depth to your answer.

Outlined below are a range of techniques that can be beneficial within the context of the T4 Case Study exam. All of them are designed to be used quickly to help generate ideas - a rapid fire approach as opposed to something to brood over.

Suitability, feasibility, acceptability

Johnson, Scholes and Whittington's model is a very common tool to use in the case study, and should provide you with a basis of your planning (as well as picking up a technical and application mark if done properly). Try to cut through any jargon, and remember the examiner is still looking for practical commercial points.

Suitability – In simple terms, looks at whether it is right for the company. Ask yourself whether it matches their strengths and whether it follows the direction of the current environment. Think about whether it could be something that would slot into the current strategy without much issue. i.e. can you see the company doing something like this?

Acceptability – looks at whether the company should do it. Here you can talk about risk, reaction and return. You may think through different stakeholders responses, or whether it fits with the current risk profile. If you have performed any calculations, the results of those can be discussed in here. i.e. do the numbers stack up?

Feasibility – looks at whether the company can actually do it. Here, think of all the specific resources required to carry out the proposal, and drill down into those. i.e. can they physically make it happen?

It is best suited to tackling a potential opportunity because:

- it provides structure to your answer, breaking it down into clearly defined sections.

- it provides focus for your points under the headings given.

A slight variation to this technique that can be applied to problems as well as opportunities is to think about strategic, financial and operational aspects (both in terms of impact and alternative solutions).

Plus, minus, interesting

The use of Johnson, Scholes & Whittington's model of suitability, feasibility and acceptability is fantastic when evaluating a proposal. However, it can take a bit longer to do, and might sometimes lead to some vague comments if there isn't much to say under a particular heading.

To speed up the process, an alternative approach is to think about advantages (**plus**), disadvantages (**minus**) and other **interesting** points relating to a proposed course of action. Since this is often quicker, it can be useful where there is more than one proposal to evaluate or where you're dealing with a lower priority issue and you have greater time pressure.

Thinking in terms of advantages and disadvantages is something that many of us do quite naturally anyway. Where the additional value is obtained within this thinking technique is in the 'interesting' element.

These will often relate to brief thoughts or ideas, maybe related to an alternative way in which something could be done, or the potential implications of a course of action. Another key 'interesting' point might relate to an ethical dilemma, and this technique is therefore very useful when you have an issue that is both a business issue and an ethical issue.

Internal v external

It's all too easy to focus on just one area in your answer whereas to maximise your mark you should try to give a balanced answer, covering a number of points. One thought process that helps you do this is a consideration of matters both internal and external to the organisation. This can help answer the question of "how should we react?"

Internal thoughts look at how we should deal with the issue away from customers or external stakeholders. It covers more 'in house' solutions. This could incorporate how we might need to change the culture, our processes or employee training.

External thoughts look at how to react in terms of dealing with customers or how to communicate with external stakeholders such as the media, or regulatory bodies.

When writing your formal answer there is no need to have separate titles for your consideration of internal and external aspects however by thinking in this way during your planning time your formal answer should be more rounded and comprehensive.

A slight variation involves basing your thoughts around Mendelow's stakeholder analysis model and consider 'other people's views'. For the issue in hand, you consider all the people affected by the issue (both internal and external stakeholders) and what their reactions or concerns are likely to be. This in turn will help to reveal the full breadth of impact of issues as well evaluate potential courses of action / recommendations to address an issue.

Short-term v long-term

Short-term impact focuses on things that will happen immediately. These are usually fairly obvious and would most likely be things you would consider without the use of this technique. However, considering the longer-term impact of an issue (for example, longer-term reputational damage, the impact on employee morale in the longer-term or perhaps a real option that you'll have or not have); these are the areas that can very often be missed.

You can also use the technique to help identify solutions:

- Short term solutions deal with the things we need to do immediately – ones that convey the sense of urgency, that deal with a quick fix. These are possibly more operational options. Due to the nature of these short terms solutions, they tend to be more reactive – an actual response to dealing with a particular problem right here and now.

- Long term solutions on the other hand, might focus on prevention e.g. how we can stop that problem from happening again. These might focus more on more proactive responses covering the strategic elements, control and leadership issues.

In my company

Try to imagine what would happen if a similar situation had occurred at your own company, or within your own team. This breaks down any barriers faced by the scenario, and puts you into a more familiar everyday place, that you feel more confident about. You can even combine this technique with the 'other people's views' technique, and ask 'what would my boss do?' or 'how would our shareholders react?'

5 Practice makes perfect

At Kaplan, we believe that the secret of success in the case study exam is to practise using mock exams. However, sitting your first mock exam can often be quite daunting. Almost like learning to drive, there seems to be so many things to remember and everything has to be done at the same time.

The rest of this chapter gives you a chance to develop your skills through a series of a mini-case scenarios. Each scenario replicates a potential paragraph out of the un-seen material and gives the sort of information you would expect to be provided with in the exam.

By working through these mini-case scenarios, getting a chance to practise different thinking techniques on different types of issues, you will feel more equipped to tackle multiple scenarios at once, within an exam environment.

Some of the answers to the scenarios contain notes to show how a thinking technique might be applied to that situation. The aim of these is to demonstrate the thought process and range of ideas that might be possible when planning your answer. These are not presented as the "correct" answer to your planning; they are just one on many suitable answers. Your planning should consist of brief notes (often that only you can understand) that can later be used to help structure and write your report.

For each scenario there is a sample answer showing the sort of thing that could have been written in the exam. These have deliberately been written in a range to styles to reflect a variety of approaches to writing your script. Before reviewing each answer you should attempt to prepare the sections of the report that you would write relating to the issue outlined.

Mini Case Scenario 1 - Possible director resignation

Since the release of the 2011 accounts for D plc, there has been a series of board room disputes.

The Sales Director, who was already disillusioned at the lack of growth in the forecast over the next three years, was the most vocal board member and felt that D had not been robust enough in both financial and strategic planning.

Other directors feel that having lived and worked in country Y for 20 years, the Sales Director's outlook on strategy was slightly different to the rest of the Board.

The Sales Director handed in his resignation last week; his contract requires him to provide 3 months notice. He is leaving to go to a competitor, who has also offered him a comparable salary, and had just announced an aggressive overseas expansion strategy.

Mini-Case Scenario 2 - Land acquisition

The Northern Region General Manager has asked for your assistance in assessing the potential of a piece of 'brownfield' land that the division is considering purchasing.

The land will cost £16 million. As an existing brownfield site, the manager is confident that planning permission will be granted for a development of 200 homes, provided a quantity of low-cost affordable housing is included alongside the more premium homes.

Although some initial discussions with the planning authorities have taken place, there is some uncertainty regarding the exact mix; this along with uncertainty over general house prices in the area means it is not possible to produce an accurate forecast of the average selling price per house. The development team have produced the following probabilities:

Selling price	£130,000	£140,000	£150,000
Probability	30%	60%	10%

D plc surveyors have also reported an inability to accurately forecast the average construction cost per house. This is not only due to the uncertainty regarding the housing mix, but also uncertainty regarding the ground conditions, which cannot be determined accurately until the site has been fully cleared. The surveyors and designers have therefore produced the following probabilities of forecast construction costs (excluding the cost of the land).

Construction costs	£30,000	£45,000	£60,000
Probability	35%	40%	25%

Due to the range of uncertainties, these probabilities are not directly linked to the house price probabilities.

In order for sufficient access to the development to be secured, D plc would also have to buy an adjacent strip of land currently owned by Mrs Grey. A valuer appointed by D plc has estimated that the fair value of the land, given the proposed use, is £400,000. Without the development, the value of the land is approximately £50,000. Mrs Grey is unaware of the value of the land she owns.

Mini-Case Scenario 3 - Bad press

The General Manager of the Northern Region recently met with a newspaper reporter from a local free newspaper. The reporter explained that he intended to run a story next week alleging that toxic material cleared from a Brownfield site, currently being developed by H, was dumped in a public landfill site without permission. The Brownfield site was originally a ball bearing manufacturer that closed in 1998. The manufacturing process used toxic solvents to clean the ball bearings prior to sale. It is these solvents that contaminated some areas of the earth on the site and required specialist removal.

Initial investigation by H confirms the existence of the toxic material in the public landfill site and also that the material, if not removed quickly, could be damaging to the local environment and population if it entered the groundwater system.

The initial site clearance contract of the Brownfield site, including the removal of the toxic material, was sub-contracted to X Ltd - a small local site clearance specialist. However after the allegations were put to the contractor they have failed to respond to any calls or emails from H.

The full cost of cleaning the land fill site, including proper disposal of the toxic material will cost £100,000 and D plc employs staff that could perform this work. This is more than the total fee paid to the contractor for the site clearance including the toxic waste disposal.

The General Manager has asked you to evaluate the options facing the company from a business perspective and to separately consider the ethical dilemma facing D plc.

Mini Case Scenario 4 - Brand confusion

An article in the property section of a regional weekend paper has recently highlighted some confusion regarding D's portfolio. One example of this concerns a four-bedroomed house design with an integral garage. This is a very popular design used on many of D's developments across the country. It is used on both H and R developments although it is called The Monarch design by H and The Prince by R. A property journalist, recognising that these two houses were both built to exactly the same design and specification, has done some price comparisons and identified that the design is currently being marketed by the two different businesses at significantly different prices. Although much of this can be attributed to differing land values, there are some examples of situations where properties on neighbouring sites are marketed at different prices.

This has highlighted to D plc that internally and externally there is some confusion regarding the different brands. The CEO of D plc believes this is due to the fact that marketing activity is carried out at central, regional and business level and believes the best way to solve the problem is through a company restructure. At a recent board meeting three options were suggested.

Option 1

The recent restructuring of the finance, human resources and IT functions appears to be working well and one option is to follow the same logic with the marketing and sales functions currently carried out by R and S. This would result in H taking responsibility for all regional activities with the exception of operations and procurement.

Option 2

The Sales Director believes it is important to maintain a certain amount of local, brand specific sales knowledge and has therefore suggested that the marketing function is provided by H but that each business retains responsibility for a sales function.

Option 3

D plc is under significant pressure to cut costs given the perceived lack of future sales growth prospects. One suggestion which the board has therefore put forward is to completely centralise the marketing activity and create a central department within D plc which provides marketing support to all aspects of the business.

Mini-Case Scenario 5 - Resource shortage

In recent years the UK has enjoyed an influx of skilled tradesmen from European countries, in particular Eastern Europe. D plc has been able to take advantage of this large supply of relatively cheap but skilled labour. Many of these tradesmen have been in the UK for several years now and a significant proportion are now choosing to move back to their home countries. There are also increasing numbers of positions available for skilled electricians on offshore oil-rigs. These are attractive jobs due to the high salaries and favourable tax position.

As such the company is currently experiencing a shortage of skilled and qualified electricians across the whole of the Eastern region. The Operations Manager of the region is particularly concerned that this is the start of a long term shortage and worries about the impact this will have on the cost of such skilled labour. This shortage of workers is affecting the company's ability to complete several developments in the area. The Operations Manager has identified two options to resolve this problem in the short term but is also aware that plans need to be made to prevent this from adversely affecting the company in the future. These options will run for the 21 week period, starting next month, which is the deadline for a medium to long term solution to be implemented.

Option 1 – pay existing contractors overtime

Contractors currently work on average 40 hours per week. There is a possibility of engaging these contractors to work longer hours but this will entail a premium of 50% over the current hourly rate of pay of £12. The Operations Manager believes that the current shortfall in manpower could be resolved if they could find an additional 20 full time, fully qualified electricians. He has confirmed that this additional time could be covered by the existing subcontractors working on sites in the region.

Option 2 – use spare resource from the Central region

The Central region currently has more sub-contractor electricians registered on their books than they are actually utilising and so spare capacity exists. These contractors would be willing to travel to the Eastern region for a total hourly rate of £13. All accommodation and travel expenses would be paid by the company and this is estimated at £180 per electrician per week.

Mini-Case Scenario 6 - Long-term supply contract

D currently uses local suppliers for raw materials such as wood, concrete and bricks. Within each regional division, the local procurement manager sources the supplier and agrees at current market rates for prices. These are taken from a preferred supplier listing (built up over a long period of time).

For the brickwork, these local suppliers offer a full range of different brick types including some specialised regional varieties such as Newco, a brick D has recently used in some of its more bespoke H branded properties. On average, D obtains a 5% discount off trade price from these local suppliers and there is usually a one week delivery period for a supply of bricks in the volume D require. The longest contract with a current supplier is for three months. Brick costs are £152m within cost of sales in the 2011 accounts, and D currently holds 20 days worth of bricks in inventory.

Following on from a procurement managers' meeting in the central region, a proposal has emerged. A national supplier of bricks – GreatBricks – had contacted the regional manager and suggested a deal to supply all the bricks for every D house nationwide. They have offered a range of options to D for the length of contract signed, ranging from one to five years.

Length of contract	% discount
1 year	8% off trade price
3 year	13% off trade price
5 year	20% off trade price

In their initial contact, GreatBricks emphasised the fact that they guarantee 12 hour delivery and work with a sophisticated JIT stock management system to enable this. GreatBricks suggest that this could reduce stock days for bricks down to five. All their bricks come from a central factory in Birmingham. Despite holding a large range of bricks, they don't stock Newco bricks.

The procurement managers have agreed to ask a management consultant to assess the option to move to the national supplier for bricks. The assessment should include calculations for any potential cost savings and how the amount of cash that is tied up in inventory may change.

Mini-Case Scenario 7 - New legislation

The demand for energy for domestic use has been growing faster than transport sector demand, and is now responsible for over 25% of carbon emissions in the UK. Considering government plans to build millions of new homes over the next decade to meet growing demand and population growth, these emissions look set to increase, and it is clear that legislative action will be required if the UK is to manage emissions down to the target set by government (currently 60% by 2050).

The Standard Assessment Procedure (SAP) is the UK Department of Energy and Climate Change's methodology for assessing and comparing the energy and environmental performance of homes. Its purpose is to provide accurate and reliable assessments of home energy performances in order to provide the information needed to develop appropriate energy and environmental policy initiatives.

SAP works by assessing how much energy a home will consume and how much carbon dioxide will be emitted in delivering a defined level of temperature and living conditions. These assessments enable a like for like comparison of home carbon emissions and energy efficiency, with each home being given a rating between 1 (poor) and 100 (good).

It has been proposed that from 2013 new legislation will require all new houses to achieve a minimum SAP rating of 80. However, this is still to be approved by Parliament and some critics are suggesting it is unlikely that this proposal will be enacted.

D's average SAP rating is currently 73. Although the properties built by H and R are marginally above the required standard, the overall rating is being pulled down by houses built under the S brand.

A lower rating can be achieved through many different measures including those which will improve insulation or maximise the efficiency of water heating systems. Some house-builders have indicated that improvements can be achieved without additional cost through new techniques and materials, e.g. using off-site or modern methods of construction using concrete panels.

The Board of D plc are keen to improve their rating in advance of the potential new legislation and would like to understand the implications of the available options before a conclusion is reached.

Mini-Case Scenario 8 - Acquisition

At a recent D plc Board meeting, the CEO highlighted a potential opportunity to the Board. A close friend of the CEO is the Managing Director (MD) of F Ltd, a house-builder based in Devon in the South-West of England. The friend has contacted the CEO to report that F Ltd is currently suffering from significant cash flow problems and is unlikely to be able to continue trading beyond the end of the year; he has asked if D plc may be interested in buying the company. D plc does not currently have any significant operations in the region.

In 2012, F Ltd took on a major development not far from Plymouth on a site located within an existing flood plain. Whilst all precautions were taken, the site was subject to flooding during the recent freak rain storms leaving the company with significant clean-up costs. Approximately 20% of the planned 200 homes had been sold subject to contract although many of the purchasers have since contacted F looking to withdraw their offers. The MD feels that a significant drop in price will be required in order to sell the houses.

In addition to this development, the only other development F Ltd has in the pipeline relates to strategic land in owns with a current book value of £40 million. However, it is thought highly likely that planning permission will be granted on this land, meaning its fair value will increase to an estimated £50 million. F Ltd was planning on developing this land throughout 2013 - 2015, building an estimated 650 homes. This land is regarded as premium and is not located in a flood plain.

F Ltd's MD has supplied D plc's CEO with the following forecast for 2013 – 2015. This forecast has been updated to reflect the current position.

	2013	2014	2015
Forecast completions	200	300	350
Average selling price (£'000)	140	160	175
Gross profit margin (%)	0%	10%	10%
Operating expenses (£m)	0.5	0.6	0.7

In addition to the above land, F Ltd is forecast to have non-current assets of £0.5m and inventory of £2 million, all of which will relate to construction work in progress on the affected site. The company has debt finance with a book value of £35m, an is expected to have an overdraft of £3 million and trade payables of £0.3m.

The MD of F Ltd has also approached another national house-builder, in addition to D plc in order to gauge their interest. He has stated however, that he believes D plc offers a better match for the business.

The Board have asked you to value the company and to appraise the potential acquisition. For the purposes of the valuation, the operating cash flows before tax are expected to equal profits from operations and no significant movements in working capital are forecast. An effective tax rate of 28% should be assumed and the Finance Director has advised that an appropriate risk adjusted cost of capital would be 15%. You should assume that any acquisition would take place at the end of 2012.

Test your understanding answers

Mini Case Scenario 1 - Possible director resignation

Walkthrough of the planning process

This is a great chance to use a particular thinking technique, just in case you hit a brick wall in the exam. 'In my company' tries to make you think of a similar situation happening at the organisation where you work, to try and then see what the options are to solve it. To illustrate this process, let's consider a similar situation arising at Kaplan, but as you read through this, try to transfer this to your company and see if you have any different ideas.

Let's imagine that a T4 tutor has just resigned after day one of the course, and has a one month notice period, meaning they will miss the later stages of the course. If you were the centre manager, what would your concerns be, and what could you do about it?

Initial thoughts (impact). This tutor has got lots of experience, which we will lose from the business. The students might love them, so it could affect our quality or reputation, especially as it's a specialised subject. If they are going to a competitor, they could take ideas, or even students with them. And we only have a month (urgency), so we need to think about this pretty quickly.

So what could we do? The centre manager would want to know the reasons why they have resigned, and whether they could actually persuade them to stay – it could have been a rash decision.

They are leaving? If they have made their mind up to leave, we need to get someone to teach the remainder of the course. This means we need a short term solution (this could even give me a heading in the exam).

Who could we get to do that? Maybe another tutor in the centre could do it. That would be the easiest solution, but T4 is a specialised subject, and maybe other tutors haven't studied the specific case study, or don't have case study experience. They might want to do it though. Maybe they are teaching on the days needed (so there's a lack of availability), or it would mean they take too much on (therefore causing them stress).

Anyone else? We could get tutor from a different centre. Again we need to check availability, but there might also be an internal charge, hence a cost to the centre.

Anywhere else we could get a tutor from? Failing all of that, we could get a freelance tutor to do the days. This would be a viable solution as there are plenty of freelance tutors looking for work, but it would cost more.

So that would solve the short term problem of dealing with the revision course. But we've still got to solve the longer term problem of replacing that tutor not only doing T4 for the next sitting – but also for other subjects they teach, or maybe they are in charge of client relations, or perform many other roles.

So how do we replace them in the longer term?

Internally? We could get a current tutor member to step up to do T4 permanently going forward. This would allow them to progress, be good motivation for them, and be a cheaper solution too.

Externally? We could recruit a new tutor from outside the business – maybe from a competitor. This would get some fresh ideas and guaranteed experienced resource. However, the recruitment process could take a long time, they might have notice periods to see out, and we might have to pay a higher salary to attract them.

Hopefully you can see how by imaging this happening in your company, one you are used to and involved with, has generated plenty of ideas, some headings, some advantages and disadvantages that you can use and then adapt to the scenario you have been given in the exam.

Have a go at it!! See how a lot of the similar ideas from above, can be used in the D scenario.

Sample solution

Impact of the problem

The Sales Director oversaw an increase in the number of completed houses in 2011, and has helped guide the business back to growth. The Sales Director will understand the mix of sales required on particular developments, and this experience will be a big loss to the business.

The risk associated with his departure is increased as he is joining a competitor. As a key member of the board, the Sales Director will be privy to confidential information that could be of great value to a competitor.

D trades solely in the UK; with house prices stabilising but the outlook still being unclear, the Sales Director will have to play a vital role in monitoring the growth figures of the company.

Alternative courses of action

Short term

The Board could try to persuade the Sales Director to stay, but having voiced his disappointment for a while and with his resignation already handed in, this is unlikely. D plc may also have to improve the terms of his contract, something they would not want to set a precedent for. Although D plc would worry about losing his knowledge of both the UK and potentially Country Y, him staying could destabilise the Board if he was demotivated and uninterested in the future of D.

His departure will reduce some of the boardroom conflict, as fellow board members may question his commitment if he was convinced to stay. D plc should insist that he works his notice period to allow a smooth hand over to his successor but could take the precaution of removing his board position and not allowing him to participate in board meetings. This will help to reduce the risk of confidential information transferring to the competitor.

A temporary replacement solution would be to promote a current employee of D plc. This could either be another director (though with only two other executive directors this may be unlikely), or to promote someone from the regional teams. This would provide a quick solution, and allow someone with knowledge of the business to step into the role.

At this important time for D plc, it could mean too much responsibility for one person to take. For another director, whose current role is very different, they may struggle with the specialist nature of being Sales Director. For a member of the Regional team (e.g. the Central Region), they may lack board level experience.

D plc could look outside of the business by recruiting a consultant, or interim sales director. This would solve any issue of shared responsibilities, but it will take a while for them to get up to speed with the business. For a listed company the size of D plc, this may be a viable option as shareholders will apply pressure for strong leadership.

Long term

For the permanent post, recruiting internally provides a cheaper, quicker and easier solution. It shows that D plc is prepared to recruit from within, and is willing to provide promotional opportunities. The key would be whether there is a suitable candidate within the sales team, as the sales director role requires a strong strategic focus. Promoting from within a Region would also leave a gap in the existing sales team that would need filling.

An external candidate will help bring new blood and fresh ideas into the company; however this should be balanced against the need for stability. Finding a suitable candidate could take a long time (potentially up to a year), and will require head hunting which could be expensive. D plc must decide whether they want someone from within the same industry (such as when former Morrisons chief executive Marc Bolland became Marks and Spencer's CEO in 2010); which is often viewed as the least risky option, or whether the sales director role could come from another industry all together.

Recommendations

Recommendations

Given the size of the company and the critical stage its life cycle, an external candidate is the best long term solution.

As a result of this decision, the short-term solution becomes more of an issue. The Sales Director should be made to work his notice period, allowing D plc three months grace. If the long term replacement cannot be found in this time, an internal candidate from the regional sales teams would be the best option.

Justification

The role is one that can be transferred across industries, and would satisfy shareholders expectations. The role requires a good strategic background especially given D plc's lack of growth predicted for the next three years.

When the Sales Director's notice period is over, appointing the Sales manager from a region gives a quicker solution, allowing an easier handover from the Sales Director, and provides some continuity for the business.

Action

Human Resources should prepare a job specification in consultation with the rest of the Board. D should consider the use of recruitment agencies that specialise at Director level appointments.

The job vacancy should be announced immediately and interested parties should be sent the job specification. Interviews should be arranged within a month and conducted by the Board.

Mini-Case Scenario 2 - Land acquisition

Walkthrough Plan

It is clear that some calculations will be required here; it will be impossible to reach a recommendation without knowing whether this site will deliver a positive return.

The existence of probabilities gives a clear indication that expected value calculations will be required. Before you begin to prepare anything, it's worth considering what level of detail is required and how the calculation is best laid out.

It would be a fairly simple calculation to work out the expected selling price per house, the expected cost, to multiply this by the number of houses and then deduct the cost of the land. This will give a quick assessment of whether the expected return is positive or not.

However, the Northern Region General Manager has asked for an assessment of the potential, and it is doubtful whether this one figure would truly deliver all the information he needs to assess the project return. After all, we know that return should be proportionate to risk, yet we won't have provided any information to help with that risk assessment.

A more detailed calculation, one which looks at the likelihood of making a loss and puts a value to the maximum amount of profit and / or loss that could be made, is therefore going to facilitate a much greater depth of discussion.

Before you perform the calculations, it might be worth thinking about what else you could discuss within your analysis. If you can think of plenty to say, then perhaps the calculations wouldn't be viewed as quite so important.

An SFA approach could be adopted or simply advantages and disadvantages. Although this may shape the structure of your answer don't confine these labels to simple headings. Regardless of whether you use them in your report, they are prompts for ideas and will allow you to view things from different perspectives.

We know that the acquisition of strategic land is a CSF. We also know that the D plc shareholders are likely to have concerns at present given the lack of forecast growth. Whenever your answer mentions shareholders or other key stakeholders, there is often an opportunity to use Mendelows matrix as a technical model to help explore the impact. Here an unhappy institutional shareholder would certainly move into the key player position meaning the directors will face more scrutiny (or could even lose their jobs). Acquiring the land would therefore be a good way to keep them happy (provided the return is good).

In terms of disadvantages, it is difficult to think of much to say without being able to comment on risk. This is therefore an indication that those calculations will be very useful.

A sample answer

Impact of the problem

Considering Mendelow's matrix assessing stakeholder interest and power, the shareholders, and in particular Institutional shareholders would normally rank within the 'keep satisfied' quadrant. Provided the company is delivering sufficient return these shareholders would be considered as having high power and low interest. However, given the recent lack of dividend and the general condition of the housing market, a failure to maintain a consistent level of house completions would undoubtedly raise their interest and move them into a 'key player' position. At this point, the Directors could find themselves facing votes of no confidence from key shareholders.

Absolutely crucial to maintaining completion levels is securing access to strategic land; this is a critical success factor of the industry.

Analysis of the proposal

Advantages

Based on the expected values calculated in the appendix, this land would be expected to deliver a return of nearly £3m gross profit, or 11%. This is before taking account of the additional strip of land that would need to be acquired from Mrs Grey (this has been discussed within the ethics section of the report).

However, if conditions were to move in D plc's favour, this return could increase to as much as £8m (or 42%).

The acquisition of this land represents a good opportunity to shore up the potential of the business by ensuring there are sufficient land banks to meet housing demand in the future. It would also help to increase the significance of the Northern region; representing approximately 10% of the number of homes completed in this region last year, this would be viewed as a sizeable development.

D plc has sufficient cash and this provides a mechanism for earning a greater return than is being earned at present.

Disadvantages

There is a 23% chance that this project could result in a gross loss when the impact of the additional strip of land is factored in (see appendix); many would view this as high risk.

However, these forecasts are just that. By the time planning permission is received and the development was about to take place, further information would be available which would allow a more informed decision regarding future actions. Many building companies are forced to impair land values: in 2008 Persimmon were forced to write down their land values by £600m, the biggest write-down in the industry at that time. As a result, six-monthly reviews for impairment are now commonplace for most house-builders given the market uncertainties.

The expected gross profit of the project is lower than was seen in 2011 (11% v 14%) and is significantly lower than the 22% forecast for 2012. Since planning permission is virtually guaranteed, this will be pushing up the acquisition price of the land, thereby restricting the return that can be earned. It is possible that D plc may prefer to invest more speculatively in 'strategic' land where there is the potential of earning much higher returns.

Recommendations

Recommendation

It is recommended that the land is purchased. For recommendations regarding the additional strip of land see the ethics section.

Justification

£16m is a relatively small investment given the amount of cash D plc currently has available. Even though there is a 23% chance of making a loss, the upside potential of returns in excess of 20%, is far greater.

Actions

The Northern Region General Manager should meet with the land owners to commence negotiations. That the land cannot be accessed properly without the additional strip of land should be used to D plc's advantage as a justification for bidding a lower amount. A further negotiating point should surround the uncertainty over ground conditions. Any reduction in the price paid will only increase the return made.

It is also recommended that D plc's surveyor and design team have further meetings with the planning authorities to see if some of the current uncertainties can be clarified. This will enable a more accurate assessment of the likely return to be made.

Appendix - Financial evaluation

Expected average selling price per house (£130,000 × 0.3 + £140,000 × 0.4 + £150,000 × 0.1) = £138,000

Total expected sales revenue (needed to calculate margin) = £138,000 × 200 homes = £27.6 million

Expected construction costs per home (£30,000 × 0.35 + £45,000 × 0.4 + £60,000 × 0.25) = £43,500

Total expected profit = £27.6 million - (£43,500 × 200 homes) - £16 million = £2.9 million

Based on expected values only, the acquisition delivers a (£2.9m ÷ £27.6m) 10.5% return.

| | Average construction costs per home | | | | | |
| | £35,000 (35%) | | £45,000 (40%) | | £60,000 (25%) | |
Avg revenue / home	£m	Prob	£m	Prob	£m	Prob
£130,000 (30%)	4.0	0.105	1.0	0.120	(2.0)	0.075
£140,000 (60%)	6.0	0.210	3.0	0.240	0	0.150
£150,000 (10%)	8.0	0.035	5.0	0.040	2.0	0.025

Note: Each '£m' column shows the profit from development after the land cost for that combination of revenue and cost. Each has been calculated as [(Avg revenue – construction costs) × 200 homes – £16m]. The 'Prob' columns show the probability of that combination arising. It has been calculated by multiplying the probabilities of each event together.

Ethics section

D plc and the Northern Region General Manager specifically face an ethical dilemma regarding their dealings with Mrs Grey to acquire the additional strip of land. Since Mrs Grey is unaware of the true value of the land, they could perhaps get away with making a very low offer (of say £50,000) and therefore improving the return on the project.

However, many would perceive this action to be unethical, taking advantage of a person's ignorance.

An alternative option would be to pay Mrs Grey the fair value of the land although this conflicts with the objective of maximisation of shareholder wealth.

Recommendation

It is recommended that the Northern Region General Manager contacts Mrs Grey to express D plc's interest in the land. If she agrees to the idea of selling in principle, she should be advised to seek professional advice regarding what she would regard as a fair price. This ensures that she has been given the opportunity to equip herself with the facts.

The success of the whole development rests on acquiring this land and so it is crucial that Mrs Grey's co-operation is gained.

Mini-Case Scenario 3 - Bad press

Walkthrough plan

This issue clearly has both a business and an ethical dimension. Before you start preparing your answer (or even get too far into your planning), it's useful to make sure you're clear about the distinction.

Business issue – weighing up the potential for reputational damage, and the lost sales that could result, against the cost of any clean up. If the risk of lost sales was felt to be low, then from a business perspective one clear option would be to 'do nothing'.

Ethical issue – does D plc have a moral duty to take responsibility for the clean-up of the toxic waste even though they had sub-contracted this to a third party?

The advice from the T4 examiner is to address all ethical issues within a separate ethics section in your report. However, the line between the business and ethical issues can be blurred and so sometimes it can be difficult to cover one without the other. In these cases, you may find it more efficient to cover the ethical issue alongside the business issue. However, only take this approach is you're really struggling for time and absolutely have to. It brings a risk that you fail to fully cover either the business or ethical issue and so therefore lose out on marks.

To analyse the business issue, a useful thought process might be internal v external:

External – risk of lost sales needs to be minimised so action needed to protect reputation, This will either involve issuing some form of press statement or liaising with the reporter writing the original article to ensure D plc's side of the story is presented.

Internal – this focuses on the processes, namely: in the short-term, what do we do about this incident (do we help with the clean up operation or not), and in the long-term, how do we prevent this sort of thing happening again.

For the ethical issue, we have to be clear to evaluate this in isolation, away from the business perspective. You also must be careful not to confuse ethical issues with legal issues. By dumping the toxic waste X Ltd have undoubtedly acted illegally, as such they are automatically in breach of their contact with D plc. What we're dealing with here is whether, after concluding that if not removed, the toxic waste would start to cause damage to the local environment and population, D plc doesn't have a moral responsibility to assist with the clean-up. You could argue that a perceived duty of care exists between a builder and the local community, or you could debate around the ethics of conflicts between stakeholders (here, the local community, X Ltd, the media and the shareholders).

A sample answer

Impact

Although the contract to remove and dispose of the toxic material on the Brownfield site was subcontracted to an external specialist firm the press report could have a negative impact on D plc's reputation and the H brand specifically. In a similar situation, Apple suffered a negative impact to its reputation following press reports of polluted waste and toxic metals being dumped by factories within its supply chain in China. Ultimately if this story is picked up and reported in the national media it could negatively impact share price of D plc.

The negative reports could also impact the perception of the business when applying for future planning permissions to local government with an increased risk of refusal or more onerous clauses attached to permissions relating to site clearance.

Internally if D plc decides to take remedial action to clean up the landfill site and dispose of the waste properly then there will be a cost impact as well the time spent by management dealing with the issue.

Analysis of alternative solutions

Three alternatives are proposed to deal with this issue.

Deny responsibility for the incident

It could be argued that as the removal of the toxic waste was subcontracted to a third party then H does not have any responsibility for the unauthorised disposal and should not bear any of the remedial costs. H could advise the reporter that the issue is the full responsibility of X Ltd and refuse to make any further comment.

If H took a more proactive approach to solving the problem it may simply fan the flames of publicity whereas by effectively doing nothing the local reporter may turn their attention to the subcontractor. It is certainly a cheap option but it does not deal with the potential risk to public health and the potential damage to reputation if it is later revealed that H knew of the problem but failed to take decisive action. There are parallels to the News International phone tapping scandal where the overall reputational damage was increased by the perceived lack of action by the parent company of the Sun newspaper when the allegations came to light internally within the organisation.

There is also an ethical aspect to this issue that is dealt with separately in section 8.

Accept some level of responsibility but do not perform remedial works

Despite the site clearance being sub-contracted it seems unreasonable that H could absolve itself completely from any responsibility. However it could make a statement acknowledging the issue and advise that it is in discussions with X Ltd to ensure it fulfils its contractual responsibilities and makes good the damage at the landfill and disposes of the toxic material in a legally approved way.

This will demonstrate that the company does recognise the issue exists and its importance. It is also a minimum cost option however the risk of reputational damage is still present especially as the subcontractor is refusing to make contact with H and the remedial cost is in excess of the initial contract price. There is a clear risk that X Ltd will not clear up the landfill site and the story continues to generate negative media coverage over a prolonged period.

Accept full responsibility for the matter and commence remedial works

The third option is for H to proactively clear the landfill site and dispose of the toxic material itself in a legal and environmentally friendly way. This would be an expensive option but this needs to be balanced against the potential negative impacts of the alternatives.

By taking responsibility H would be complying with and possibly exceeding best practice corporate social responsibility principles.

Recommendations

Recommendation

It is recommended that H immediately commences a cleanup operation to remove the toxic material from the landfill site and dispose of it in a legal authorised manner. It should also seek to recover any costs incurred from X Ltd. It should also issue a statement to the local reporter explaining the actions that are to be taken by H to resolve the issue and thanking the reporter for bringing the matter to their attention.

Internally a review of subcontracting contracts and control procedures should be initiated across D plc to learn from this issue and prevent such an incident occurring in the future.

Justification

The potential external reputation damage that this issue could cause exceeds the remedial cost especially as some or all of the costs may be recoverable from X Ltd.

Dealing with such an issue in a proactive and positive manner can actually enhance the reputation of a business. If the toxic material were left for any extended period of time and human health was impacted then regulatory penalties and litigation from affected individuals would be likely to far exceed the cleanup costs.

Actions to be taken

H to immediately instruct the clean-up operation to begin using D plc internal staff. Contact should be made with X Ltd informing them of this decision and requesting that they assist with the cleanup operation.

A formal negotiation process should be initiated with X Ltd to seek compensation for the cleanup costs incurred by H. This may lead to potential legal action against X Ltd for breach of contract and damages.

H marketing should draft a press statement for release to the local reporter. The statement should be approved at D plc board level before release.

D plc internal audit team should be instructed to plan a systems and control review of subcontractor operations. The plan should be agreed by the audit committee of D plc.

D plc audit committee should investigate the need to voluntarily report the unauthorised disposal to the relevant regulatory authority.

Ethical section

Why this is an ethical issue

The ethical issue is whether H has a moral responsibility to make good the damage caused by the actions of the sub-contractor X Ltd.

For H to be seen to be acting with integrity it is likely that some moral responsibility exists and it cannot simply deny any responsibility. The D plc board seeks to comply with best practice corporate governance and this must include the acceptance of responsibility to stakeholders for the actions of the business and this must include, to some greater or lesser extent, the action of its subcontractors.

Recommendations for this ethical issue

Doing nothing or denying responsibility is not an option from an ethical perspective as H must take responsibility for its actions. It is recommended that the only viable ethical option is to commence immediate remedial works and then seek assistance and/or compensation from X Ltd for the cost of the operations.

Mini Case Scenario 4 - Brand confusion

Plan

Impact	Technical and Diversity
• strong brand image for each of the businesses - easily recognisable by the customer. • customers unwilling to pay the prices charged	• Marketing mix - brand = product and market segmentation • Persimmon's portfolio
Option 1 • cost savings. • H to exercise some control over the marketing effort • conflict • lack of understanding within H's current marketing team regarding the other brands local knowledge is vital **Option 2** • This would have similar benefits and problems to option 2 • satisfy the Sales Directors objection **Option 3** • significant change in the overall structure of the organisation • all brands are controlled from a group perspective • most cost effective solution • local staff - local needs • animosity following restructure.	**Recommendation** • option 2 is accepted **Justification** • logical next step following the restructure of the other function • balance of control and local knowledge **Actions to be taken** • board approval • consultation process • HR director of D plc drawing up a detailed plan for the restructure new team is fully briefed on the branding strategy.

A sample answer

Impact

The marketing function of an organisation such as D plc is primarily responsible for creating and developing interest in the properties and sites which the company is building. It is then the responsibility of the sales teams to negotiate with individual customers. It is vital that the marketing department create a strong brand image for each of the businesses that will be easily recognisable by the customer.

Brand is a core element of product within the marketing mix. It is perfectly possible and commercial for a house-builder to offer brands at different price points. The Persimmon group of companies also includes the Charles Church premium brand and Westbury Properties social housing and is very successful in what they do. However, when attempting to segment the market in this way, it is even more important to ensure a clear brand identify and distinction is the marketing mix is to be effective. The impact of the brand confusion within D plc could lead to customers being unwilling to pay the prices charged, particularly for the premium homes built by H.

Analysis of alternative course of action

Option 1

By incorporating the sales and marketing function into the H business, D plc would benefit from the resulting cost savings. It would also allow H to exercise some control over the marketing effort and therefore hopefully prevent some of the disparities in pricing and branding that have occurred recently.

This could however create conflict as the Managing Director of each business will be responsible for their own profits and the Managing Director of H could be accused of focusing the attention of the marketing department on H properties to the detriment of the other businesses. There may also be a lack of understanding within H's current marketing team regarding the other brands within the D group.

Furthermore the Sales Director is correct in believing that local knowledge is vital when selling houses. It would be difficult to ensure that local knowledge could be adequately utilised if sales was managed from within H rather than by each business.

Option 2

Alternatively D could maintain a sales function within each business and only move the marketing activity to H. This would have similar benefits and problems to option 2 but would satisfy the Sales Directors objection that selling homes needs to be managed at a local level.

Option 3

The final option involves a more radical restructure to create a centralised function providing marketing support and expertise to all regions and businesses within D plc. The group currently has no services provided at such a central level so this represents a significant change in the overall structure of the organisation.

This option would ensure that all brands are controlled from a group perspective and could lead to the most appropriate and commercial decisions being made about each brand without the complication of individual divisional goals. It could also represent the most cost effective solution.

If this option is implemented it would be important to ensure that the group marketing team fully appreciate the different brands which D plc offers and continue to interact with local staff to ensure local needs are taken into account. This could prove difficult to begin with as some animosity is likely to remain following a restructure.

Another difficulty could arise with maintaining the level of local knowledge, and tailoring the marketing to those local differences. This is something that the Board currently view as a critical success factor.

Recommendations

Recommendation

It is recommended that option 2 is accepted and the marketing function is provided to all businesses by H.

Justification

This is a logical next step following the restructure of the other functions at business level. It provides a balance of some central control over the different brand images whilst still enabling some local knowledge to form part of the marketing activity.

Actions to be taken

This restructure will first need board approval. Once this is obtained the company will need to begin a consultation process with those staff affected by such a restructure to ensure all views are aired and considered. The first stage in the consultation process will involve the HR director of D plc drawing up a detailed plan for the restructure and communicating this to those concerned.

The regional HR managers will need to ensure that all staff are aware of the plan and try to explain and reassure them that this plan is in the best interests of the company. They will need to communicate with the rest of the business to try and ensure that alternative positions are identified for any staff at risk of redundancy and where possible these staff should be offered any new positions created within H.

The Marketing Director will then need to ensure that the new team is fully briefed on the branding strategy of the group and together they should draw up a plan for implementing this strategy.

Mini-Case Scenario 5 - Resource shortage

Plan

Impact	Technical and Diversity
• delays = cost (knock on effect). • loss of sales • unhappy customers	• Tech = Porter's Five Forces (power of suppliers) • Diversity = any disruption (Thailand floods?)
Pros and cons of options **Option 1** • easier • site knowledge / flexibility. • cost? • concern over working time directive / H&S / quality **Option 2** • Calc - hours plus exps v option 1 • Difficulty in co-ordinating between regions • reduce power of existing subs • Sensitivity - on difference in cost • Capacity okay • Don't know development	**Recommendation** • option 1 (use existing) is accepted **Justification** • Site knowledge = less problems • normal business practice • more flexible • will increase motivation **Actions to be taken** **Short-term** • Contact existing subs with offer of overtime • Produce schedule **Long-term** • Need to prevent again • Recruit more subs • Set up / sponsor apprenticeship scheme.

Impact

It is important for D plc to have all tradesmen available on site when needed as delays in completing one part of the process can have a knock on effect on the next stages. For example the plasterers will not be able to complete their work until all electrical work has been completed and checked. These delays will have a significant impact on the overall cost of completing a development as they will be paying tradesmen for idle time.

This was seen in Thailand during the floods of 2011, where shortages from lack of sand meant that several building projects had to stop temporarily.

Delays will also potentially mean that homes are not ready for occupation on the date which has been agreed with the purchaser. This will cause bad feeling with the customers and also have an impact on D's reputation for timely completion. This could affect future sales of properties.

If the delays are severe it could mean that unsold developments, or parts of developments are not ready to view for the peak Autumn buying season which could have serious cash flow implications for the company over the Winter.

Analysis of alternative courses of action

Option 1

It is possible for the region to use existing sub-contractors and pay them a premium for working overtime. This is a simple option which will have minimum administrative complications and will be easy to arrange. These electricians will be familiar with the area and with the sites involved, making the logistics of the solution more workable. In the current economic climate the ability to earn extra money is likely to be welcomed by the sub-contractors and this could enhance the motivation of the teams on site.

This option is more expensive (£8,400) than using resource from elsewhere and would result in a total additional cost of £302,400 (see appendix). The financial difference is however only marginal, and therefore carries less weight in the decision in light of the operational benefits the option brings.

The company need to be careful however that they are not inadvertently flouting employment law. As part of the EU, the UK is bound by the Working Time Directive which states that no employee should work more than 48 hours per week, calculated over a 12 week reference period. Although it is possible for employees to opt out of this requirement it is important that D plc ensure any appropriate action is taken to ensure they are complying with all relevant laws and regulations. D plc also have an ethical duty to ensure that anyone working on their sites (whether employed or not) are not working too many hours and potentially risking their safety.

The company also needs to be mindful that allowing workers to be on site for excessive amounts of time could affect the quality of work produced which could result in incurring future rectification costs if mistakes are made.

Option 2

Using Porter's Five Forces analysis we can see that in this case the suppliers of sub-contracted skilled labour are able to exert power over the company by demanding a substantial premium to work additional hours. Using available resource from the Central region would reduce this power and show that the company has alternatives to paying expensive overtime.

By incorporating the additional expenses incurred for accommodation and travel it can be seen that as the hourly rate is lower for this option, the total cost is marginally lower at £294,000 (see appendix). An upward movement in expenses of only £20 week would see both options cost the same, so this must be carefully monitored.

This option would also require a degree of coordination between the two regions and this is something that has historically been difficult within D plc.

Recommendation

Recommendation

It is recommended that the Operations Manager of the Eastern region negotiates with the sub-contractors to complete the work using existing workers and paying an overtime premium.

Justification

This is the simplest option and normal business practice in the industry. The company should have a sufficient large pool of electricians that the additional hours can be shared out and therefore not place undue pressure on any one individual.

The existing subcontractors all have knowledge of the sites and work flows on the sites they're currently working on and so this option should be the smoothest, with the least chance of problems arising.

Actions to be taken

Short term

The Operations Director should contact the electricians currently working within the Eastern Region and ask for expressions of interest in additional hours. A schedule can then be drawn up by each site manager to ensure on time completion of each development.

Long term

It is important that plans are made to prevent, where possible, such resource issues from affecting the company in the future.

D plc should speak to specialist agencies with a view to recruiting more skilled labour from overseas. A job description should be drawn up by the HR director and adverts placed in overseas trade publications. This should be done as soon as possible to ensure that additional resource is available to start work from the target date.

The HR Director should also investigate the possibility of setting up an Apprenticeship scheme to enable D plc to train and develop its own workforce in the skills it needs for the future.

Appendix

Option 1

Cost : 21 weeks × 40 hours × £12 × 1.5 × 20 staff equivalent = £302,400

Option 2

Cost : 21 weeks × 40 hours × £13 × 20 staff equivalent = £218,400
Expenses : £180 × 21 weeks × 20 staff equivalent = £ 75,600
Total cost = £294,000

Mini-Case Scenario 6 - Long-term supply contract

Impact

With D forecasting no growth in revenue over the next three years, this places importance on finding cost savings throughout the business to ensure current levels of profitability. The sourcing of supplies has already been identified by NN (non exec director) as an area D are behind competitors so any improvements are welcome.

By agreeing to a longer term deal, D can obtain cost savings of £4.8m, £12.8m or £24m (see Appendix) depending on the length of the contract, creating a good opportunity to improve or at least maintain margins. Applying these savings to 2011 figures, this would equate to 3.6%, 9.7% or 18.2% of operating profit.

Porter's Value Chain tries to identify areas within a business that can add value, assessing both primary and support activities and creating linkages within your own organisation and throughout the whole supply chain.

Procurement is a support activity that looks at adding value in the process of buying everything, which in the case of D would including sourcing of the raw materials. Bricks are a crucial component of house building though, and the quality of supply must not be compromised by cost.

Advantages

The discounts offered by GreatBricks are on a sliding scale, improving greatly for the 5 year deal. With up to £24m savings on current brick costs, this will free up cash for investment in more strategic land. Further financial benefits of having a shorter stock cycle include reduced stock holding, which provides modest positive cash impact of £6.31m for a one year deal (this rises to £6.58m for the 5 year deal).

By having a guaranteed 12 hour delivery option, this will help with the operations of all our current and future house building projects enhancing the reputation of D for building projects to time. In addition, this will reduce any idle time on site by creating a much more efficient supply chain. With less stock around, it may even reduce the risk of on-site theft, a common (though smaller) risk in this industry.

Dealing with only one company will mean less management time in terms of sourcing, negotiating and managing this aspect of the supply chain. Having good relationship with a key, reliable supplier is very beneficial in an industry with so many potential suppliers. For example, GAP group recently secured a two year sole supplier status for plant and tool hire to Glasgow council construction arm City Building.

Disadvantages

The main disadvantage is that GreatBricks cannot fulfil the criteria for the full variety of bricks needed by D, especially for the H brand. To ensure that H houses can still be built to the standards required, D will have to pay higher prices for smaller volumes from local suppliers. This could force D to concentrate on some of the smaller valued properties in terms of housing mix on new developments. It may also mean that D may fail to win some planning permission on strategic land due to not having enough 'high end' houses.

Being tied into a longer deal (especially an unprecedented 5 year deal), would increase the power of the main supplier GreatBricks as D would be reliant on them. If GreatBricks were to fail to deliver on their promises of speed and quality, this could have implications for the rest of the supply chain. The inflexibility of this new procurement policy, coupled with any broken relationships with historic suppliers could lead to full market prices being paid in instances where GreatBricks have not delivered.

By having just one national warehouse, this increases the carbon footprint of each house built, something which goes against the pressures put on the house building industry to reduce the carbon emissions.

By entering into a long term deal with an unknown supplier, there could be doubts over the quality provided. This issue may not be known until way into the contract, and erode D's reputation for good quality homes.

Other issues

Regardless of length of contract entered into, D will face a problem of co-ordinating the requirements that are needed across all regions given there is not a centralised IT system. This will cause logistics issues, errors on ordering and management time in resolving disputes.

Recommendations

Recommendations

It is recommended that before any long term contract is signed, a trial period with the new supplier is requested. This could cover a 3 month period in the Central region and would therefore affect a much smaller volumes than the original proposal.

This will also give GreatBricks time to source the Newco bricks that are required by D. If that is successful and all of D's requirements can be met, then a 5-year contract would be the most suitable option to enter into.

If GreatBricks cannot provide Newco bricks, then Procurement must still maintain current suppliers of that product type in the relevant geographic regions.

If such savings are available for national contracts, it is recommended that a review of all current contracts is performed on all raw material suppliers.

Justification

The risks of disruption in the supply chain are too great to tie into such a significant contract for a long period of time with an unknown supplier. Adding value comes by building relationships over time, something D have previously done.

The Central region would allow any trial the best chance to succeed by having the national supplier main warehouse nearby. Any issues or errors could be solved with minimal disruption to the rest of the business.

A discount under the 5-year option provides an additional annual saving of £11.2m; a total of £56m over the life of the contract. This is significantly more than the discount under the 3 year contract.

Action

The Operations Director for the Central region must contact GreatBricks in the next few weeks to put forward a proposal for a trial period. This could build D's initial relationship but maintain our current supply chain.

If the trial period is successful, then Procurement should look to draw up contracts for the 5-year supply. Negotiations will also include service level agreements on meeting quality, delivery and range. Of particular importance will be agreeing a clear definition of 'trade price' that would prevent GreatBricks from artificially increasing their prices over and above those of their competitors. This would ensure that over the course of the agreement, D plc was always receiving a competitive deal.

Procurement should also look into the possibility of inserting exit clauses on failure to deliver D's requirements.

The Operations and Procurement teams should conduct some research into whether other suppliers of raw materials could supply on a national basis. This report should be presented to the Board in the next 2 months.

Appendix

Current costs £152m after a 5% discount = £160m trade price

COS figure based on contract length

1 year (8% discount) ; £160m @ 8% discount = £147.2m
3 year (13% discount) ; £160m @ 13% discount = £139.2m
5 year (20% discount) ; £160m @ 20% discount = £128m

Annual Savings

1 year £152m – £147.2m = £4.8m
3 year £152m – £139.2m = £12.8m
5 year £152m – £128m = £24m

Stock calculations

Current brick stock = 20/365 days × £152m = £8.33m

1 year deal : 5/365 × £147.2m = £2.02m (therefore stock lowered by £6.31m)
2 year deal : 5/365 × £139.2m = £1.91m (therefore stock lowered by £6.42m)
5 year deal : 5/365 × £128m = £1.75m   (therefore stock lowered by £6.58m)

Mini-Case Scenario 7 - New legislation

Impact

D plc have built a strong brand with a reputation for quality homes. From a PESTEL analysis it is clear that regulation is a key factor in this industry and so it is imperative that these homes are fully compliant with all relevant legislation for D to maintain their reputation. Failure to respond to these planned changes could lead to customers choosing alternative, more environmentally sound developments.

It is important for a company like D to ensure they are always aware of forthcoming legislation and develop strategy to incorporate changes. They should also try to anticipate other legislative changes which may occur. In 2008 the UK introduced the Energy Act which gave home owners the chance to install solar panels and set off the cost of installation against income from the energy generated. Many companies developed strategies to take advantage of this by installing solar panels for free and then contracting with the customer to receive the income generated, but only those who anticipated the changes to the legislation (and the subsequent reduction in tariffs) have been able to fully benefit.

Analysis of alternative courses of action

Option 1

One option is to ignore the impending legislative changes and continue to build homes in the same way; this will be the simplest option from an operational perspective and won't involve any additional costs. If the legislation fails to get through Parliament, this approach will be regarded, with the benefit of hindsight, as the most sensible. However, if the new limits are enacted, and D plc is unable to comply, the company could face potential fines and reputational damage. It is possible that mortgage companies might refuse to lend money to customers wishing to buy a new home that doesn't meet the required standard. This would leave D with homes that are virtually impossible to sell and the financial impact would be severe. The potential negative publicity could be incredibly damaging.

Failure to prepare a strategy beforehand increases the chances that D plc would not be able to comply with any new legislation immediately.

Option 2

Alternatively D could choose to ensure all new homes built by D meet the required standards by installing good quality insulation and high specification heating systems to the current house designs. This would ensure that D is able to continue to pursue a strategy of high quality homes and is not subject to any penalties arising from non-compliance.

From a financial perspective this would be an expensive option and it is not certain that the additional costs could be passed on to the customers as they may not perceive the improvements as adding significant value to the property. It would also take time to identify the most appropriate systems to install and this would need to be determined well in advance of the 2013 deadline.

Option 3

D could investigate the possibility of using modern methods of construction (MMC) involving pre-fabricated concrete systems to improve the energy efficiency of its homes. This would have the added advantage of reducing the overall costs of construction in the long term and would also make project planning significantly easier due to the amount of construction that could be completed off site.

D has no experience in this area and so this option would involve a steep learning curve. It may not be possible for D to implement this strategy in advance of the 2013 deadline.

Recommendations

Recommendation

In the short to medium-term, it is recommended that D pursue Option 1 and look to revise their house designs to incorporate sufficient insulation and improved heating systems to ensure their homes meet the potential new legislation from 2013. However, alongside this D should also look to develop expertise in MMC techniques, as outlined in option 3.

Justification

Whilst the adoption of MMC offers the best long-term solution to both reducing costs and improving energy efficiency, D must be pragmatic about their ability to utilise these methods in time for the potential legislative changes. Although option 1 would be the most expensive, it is vital that D is seen to embrace the legislation and build quality homes which are also energy efficient; this therefore provides a temporary solution to help protect D's brand reputation.

If the legislation fails to go through Parliament, the use of the revised designs could be suspended but the adoption of MMC should still be pursued given the cost savings available.

Actions to be taken

The Procurement Managers should speak to existing suppliers about obtaining the materials required. If they are not available from existing suppliers then a specification should be drawn up and discussed with alternative suppliers. It is vital that good quality materials are used for this strategy.

The S brand Managing Directors should also instruct architects to consider whether any minor changes in house design are required to improve the ventilation within new properties or facilitate installation of the insulation.

Mini-Case Scenario 8 - Acquisition

Logic of the proposal

Valuing a business is more of an art than a science; much will depend on the details of the situation. As a prospective purchaser we would obviously be looking to secure the acquisition for the lowest possible price, and the situation in which F Ltd finds itself presents an excellent opportunity to negotiate a good deal.

If we consider the net asset value of the business, this has a book value of £4.2 million (see appendix). However, the true value could be significantly higher, especially considering the imminent conversion of the strategic land into short-term land with planning permission, which is expected to increase the fair value by £10 million.

A discounted cash flow approach based on the forecast trading to 2015 shows a net present value of just over £4.4 million (see appendix). However, it must be remembered that the profit forecast over the next few years will be primarily driven by the increase in the value of the land-bank mentioned above.

Analysis of the proposal

The proposed acquisition can be analysed using Johnson, Scholes and Whittington's framework of suitability, feasibility and acceptability.

Suitability

That D plc does not currently have any significant operations in this region makes this proposal suitable as it will help to improve the geographical coverage of the company. Since local knowledge is a critical success factor in the industry, the acquisition would give D plc access to that knowledge and form a base for further expansion.

Feasibility

D plc currently has at least £112 million of cash and so financing this acquisition would not be a problem. The company's expertise in house design will transfer well to this new region given the limited differences expected.

Consideration would need to be given to how this new operation would be managed and where it would fit in the organisational structure. It would be important to retain the services of existing employees in order to secure the local insight needed.

Acceptability

An acquisition will only be acceptable is sufficient return can be gained to compensate the shareholders for the risks arising. The discounted cash flow technique of valuation is the technically superior method of valuation and this would imply returns from F Ltd over the next few years of £4.4 million. The return to D plc will be the difference between this and the acquisition price. F Ltd may argue that this valuation fails to take account of any future developments. However, with no additional land in their land bank, coupled with the fact that the lack of repeat purchase means an established customer base is of no significant value in this industry, this argument is not a strong one.

On the risk side, there is the potential reputational damage which could come from being associated with the existing flood plain development. If any of the D plc brands were to be linked with this development, sales across the rest of the UK could suffer. There is also the risk that the strategic land may fail to get planning permission or that the forecasts regarding the number of houses sold and the average selling price may not transpire.

Recommendations

Recommendation

It is recommended that D plc makes an offer of £4 million for F Ltd. The existing development should continue under the F Ltd brand but the new development should be based around the existing D plc brands with the mix being determined by the specifics of the site.

Justification

The opportunity to expand into a new region does present a good platform for future growth of the D plc brands and access to the knowledge and expertise of existing employees will help drive this growth. This goes someway to offset the potential risks.

An offer of £4m will help to ensure that D plc still sees a reasonable return from this investment. They could be prepared to pay anything up to £4.4 million as part of negotiations but should not go higher than this. Any argument regarding the additional value in the land bank when planning permission is obtained should be rejected on the grounds of uncertainty and the impact this would have on the future realised margins within the business.

By ensuring the existing development continues to be marketed under the F Ltd brand, D plc will reduce the risk of any damage to their existing brands should further problems arise.

Actions

After being approved by the Board, the Finance Director should contact the MD of F Ltd with an initial offer of £4m. The CEO should not be involved in the negotiations considering the friendship that exists.

The offer should be made subject to the completion of site surveys for both the existing development and the strategic site. This should include an estimate of the costs to complete the development, which can be compared with the forecasts provided by F Ltd.

A D plc manager with responsibility for planning applications should also contact the local planning department in Devon to enquire about the progress of the application and to assess the likelihood of permission being granted.

Appendix

Net asset value:	**£m**
Land	40.0
Non-current assets	0.5
Inventory	2.0
	_____
Total assets	42.5
Less: debt	35.0
Less: overdraft	3.0
Less: trade payables	0.3
	_____
Net asset value	4.2
	_____

Discounted cash flows:	2013	2014	2015
Revenue (Avg selling price × completions) (£m)	28.0	48.0	61.3
Gross profit (revenue × GPM) (£m)	0.0	4.8	6.1
Operating expenses (£m)	0.5	0.6	0.7
Profit from operations (£m)	-0.5	4.2	5.4
Tax (@ 28%) (£m)	0	1.2	1.5
Profit for the year (£m)	-0.5	3.0	3.9
Discount factor @ 15%	0.870	0.756	0.658
Present value (£m)	-0.44	2.29	2.57

Requirement 1(b)

Chapter learning objectives

By the end of this chapter you will have:

- Developed a better understanding of the range of documents that could be requested in requirement 1(b);
- Had a chance to practise producing each type of document in order to hone your skills

1 The scope of the secondary task

The scope of the secondary task will be restricted to either a short slide presentation, an e-mail, a draft letter or an e-mail / letter / presentation with a graph or chart attached.

It will relate to one or more of the key business issues highlighted within the unseen, although not necessarily the highest priority issue. It could relate to an ethical issue.

You must remember that above all else, this document is a **communication** document. The examiner is testing your ability to be able to communicate in an effective and appropriate way using a medium other than a report.

Slide presentation

If a slide presentation is called for, your answer need only consist of the bullet points that would appear on each slide. Read the requirement carefully as guidance will be given on how many slides to prepare and / or the maximum number of bullet points. Most likely this would be 2 slides, with a maximum of 5 bullets on each slide, or 10 bullet points in total. It is unlikely that you would need to prepare speaker notes.

You do not need to layout your answer as a slide (i.e. you don't need to draw a box). Simply noting the bullets will be sufficient.

If you are sitting the computer based exam, the use of PowerPoint to prepare slides is not allowed; instead you should include the contents of your presentation within either your Word or Excel document.

An e-mail

A requirement to draft an e-mail may be in response to a specific question raised by an individual within the unseen information, or perhaps even in response to an e-mail that is presented within the unseen.

Again, your answer should be presented after the end of your report (either on paper or in Word if sitting the computer exam).

You will need to ensure you give your e-mail a title and make it clear who it is to and who it is from. Very often guidance is given on the length of the document (for example 10 short sentences) and you'll be marked down if you don't adhere to these guidelines. You will also be marked down if you use short bullet points when the e-mail should include whole sentences.

A letter

Exactly the same as for an e-mail but laid out in letter format. That means you should include a space for an address, a date, state who the letter is addressed to and some form summary of what the letter is regarding.

The letter should be signed off in the normal business fashion, unless you are told otherwise.

Chart or graph

If requirement 1(b) calls for a chart or graph, it will most likely be as an attachment within an e-mail or as an addition to a letter or presentation. It is therefore important to recognise that marks will be earned for the content of the e-mail / letter / presentation as well as the chart or graph.

If you are sitting your exam on a computer, you should draw your chart or graph within Excel. If you are unsure how to do this, see the Quick Reference Guides available to Kaplan registered students on EN-gage or visit www.microsoft.com to download their free help sheets.

If you are sitting a paper exam, you will be provided with graph paper on which to draw your chart or graph.

In either instance, you must make sure that the axes are correctly labelled, that your chart has a title, that you include data labels showing the values you have plotted and that you provide a key.

2 Content of the secondary requirement

Regardless of what form your response to the secondary requirement needs to take, it is likely that the content or focus of it will be fairly similar.

This requirement is testing your ability to extract the most important points and to present these in a clear and succinct way. So whether it is slides, an e-mail, a letter or a chart, you must focus on who you are writing to, what they will be most concerned about and ensure you cover those points, and those alone. Of particular importance is the tone you adopt in your communication. You may need to be persuasive or conciliatory for example, depending on the situation, and getting this tone right is the key to scoring high marks.

Remember, requirement 1(b) only scores within the logic criterion. You should therefore focus your points on giving clear advice, stating opinions and providing recommendations, along with appropriate justifications (for example the output of key calculations).

You must take care not to just repeat the information you have presented within your report. Remember, this requirement is about pulling out the most important aspects and **communicating** them effectively and appropriately.

You will sometimes have to go above and beyond what you have included in your report, perhaps providing some recommendations or advice on background factors to consider.

The following exercises provide you with some examples relevant to the current case (building on some of the scenarios presented in the previous chapter). Work through each in turn before you review the sample answer at the back of the chapter.

Exercise 1 - An e-mail

In chapter 7 you were presented with the following scenario:

In recent years the UK has enjoyed an influx of skilled tradesmen from European countries, in particular Eastern Europe. D plc has been able to take advantage of this large supply of relatively cheap but skilled labour. Many of these tradesmen have been in the UK for several years now and a significant proportion are now choosing to move back to their home countries. There are also increasing numbers of positions available for skilled electricians on offshore oil-rigs. These are attractive jobs due to the high salaries and favourable tax position.

As such the company is currently experiencing a shortage of skilled and qualified electricians across the whole of the Eastern region. The Operations Manager of the region is particularly concerned that this is the start of a long term shortage and worries about the impact this will have on the cost of such skilled labour. This shortage of workers is affecting the company's ability to complete several developments in the area. The Operations Manager has identified two options to resolve this problem in the short term but is also aware that plans need to be made to prevent this from adversely affecting the company in the future. These options will run for the 21 week period, starting next month, which is the deadline for a medium to long term solution to be implemented.

Option 1 – pay existing contractors overtime

Contractors currently work on average 40 hours per week. There is a possibility of engaging these contractors to work longer hours but this will entail a premium of 50% over the current hourly rate of pay of £12. The Operations Manager believes that the current shortfall in manpower could be resolved if they could find an additional 20 full time, fully qualified electricians. He has confirmed that this additional time could be covered by the existing subcontractors working on sites in the region.

Option 2 – use spare resource from the Central region

The Central region currently has more sub-contractor electricians registered on their books than they are actually utilising and so spare capacity exists. These contractors would be willing to travel to the Eastern region for a total hourly rate of £13. All accommodation and travel expenses would be paid by the company and this is estimated at £180 per electrician per week.

Requirement

In addition to the analysis in your report for part (a), you are required to prepare an e-mail to the Eastern Region General Manager on the current shortage of qualified electricians.

Your e-mail should contain no more than 10 brief sentences, covering both financial and operational issues, including your recommendation.

Exercise 2 - An e-mail with graph / chart attached

In chapter 7 you were presented with the following scenario:

D currently uses local suppliers for raw materials such as wood, concrete and bricks. Within each regional division, the local procurement manager sources the supplier and agrees at current market rates for prices. These are taken from a preferred supplier listing (built up over a long period of time).

For the brickwork, these local suppliers offer a full range of different brick types including some specialised regional varieties such as Newco, a brick D has recently used in some of its more bespoke H branded properties. On average, D obtains a 5% discount off trade price from these local suppliers and there is usually a one week delivery period for a supply of bricks in the volume D require. The longest contract with a current supplier is for three months. Brick costs are £152m within cost of sales in the 2011 accounts, and D currently holds 20 days worth of bricks in inventory.

Following on from a procurement managers' meeting in the central region, a proposal has emerged. A national supplier of bricks – GreatBricks – had contacted the regional manager and suggested a deal to supply all the bricks for every D house nationwide. They have offered a range of options to D for the length of contract signed, ranging from one to five years.

Length of contract	% discount
1 year	8% off trade price
3 year	13% off trade price
5 year	20% off trade price

In their initial contact, GreatBricks emphasised the fact that they guarantee 12 hour delivery and work with a sophisticated JIT stock management system to enable this. GreatBricks suggest that this could reduce stock days for bricks down to five. All their bricks come from a central factory in Birmingham. Despite holding a large range of bricks, they don't stock Newco bricks.

Requirement

Prepare an e-mail to the Board, discussing the proposal to switch to the national supplier for bricks.

Your email should contain no more than 5 brief sentences, including your recommendation, and 1 chart (a column chart or a bar chart or a line graph).

The chart, an attachment to your e-mail, should show the cost comparison of the new supplier contract terms to our existing arrangements.

Exercise 3 - A letter

In chapter 7 you were presented with the following scenario:

Since the release of the 2011 accounts for D plc, there has been a series of board room disputes.

The Sales Director, who was already disillusioned at the lack of growth in the forecast over the next three years, was the most vocal board member and felt that D had not been robust enough in both financial and strategic planning.

Other directors feel that having lived and worked in country Y for 20 years, the Sales Director's outlook on strategy was slightly different to the rest of the Board.

The Sales Director handed in his resignation last week; his contract requires him to provide 3 months notice period. He is leaving to go to a competitor, who has also offered him a comparable salary, and had just announced an aggressive overseas expansion strategy.

Requirement

Draft a letter to the Sales Director from the CEO in response to his resignation. Your letter should make it clear to the Sales Director the future steps to be taken by all parties.

The letter should include clear justified actions and contain no more than 10 sentences.

Exercise 4 - A presentation

In chapter 7 you were presented with the following scenario:

An article in the property section of a regional weekend paper has recently highlighted some confusion regarding D's portfolio. One example of this concerns a four-bedroomed house design with an integral garage. This is a very popular design used on many of D's developments across the country. It is used on both H and R developments although it is called The Monarch design by H and The Prince by R. A property journalist, recognising that these two houses were both built to exactly the same design and specification, has done some price comparisons and identified that the design is currently being marketed by the two different businesses at significantly different prices. Although much of this can be attributed to differing land values, there are some examples of situations where properties on neighbouring sites are marketed at different prices.

This has highlighted to D plc that internally and externally there is some confusion regarding the different brands. The CEO of D plc believes this is due to the fact that marketing activity is carried out at central, regional and business level and believes the best way to solve the problem is through a company restructure. At a recent board meeting three options were suggested.

Option 1

The recent restructuring of the finance, human resources and IT functions appears to be working well and one option is to follow the same logic with the marketing and sales functions currently carried out by R and S. This would result in H taking responsibility for all regional activities with the exception of operations and procurement.

Option 2

The Sales Director believes it is important to maintain a certain amount of local, brand specific sales knowledge and has therefore suggested that the marketing function is provided by H but that each business retains responsibility for a sales function.

Option 3

D plc is under significant pressure to cut costs given the perceived lack of future sales growth prospects. One suggestion which the board has therefore put forward is to completely centralise the marketing activity and create a central department within D plc which provides marketing support to all aspects of the business.

Requirement

In addition to your analysis in your report for part (a), you have been asked to draft a presentation to the Board, outlining the importance and relevance of branding to D plc. Your presentation should also cover how your recommended organisational structure will assist the company to effectively promote its brands.

Your presentation should contain no more than 10 bullet points, including your recommendations.

Test your understanding answers

Exercise 1 - An e-mail

To: General Manager – Eastern region
From: An accountant
Date: Today
Subject: Shortage of electricians

It is recommended that the Operations Manger for the Eastern region negotiates with the sub-contractors to complete the work using existing workers and paying an overtime premium.

This would result in a total additional cost of £302,400 which is marginally higher than using labour from the Central region.

Despite the higher cost, it was felt that this was the simplest option and normal business practice in the industry.

By offering more work to our current suppliers, this will help build relationships with our subcontractors even more.

As we have found from recent economic downturns, suppliers appreciate the security of work we can provide for them. In addition, this will also work for us in times of crisis as our supplier will be more willing to help out.

As these electricians will be familiar with the area and specifically the sites involved, there will reduced risk of mistakes, and this will retain our efficiency in house building in the Eastern area.

Although you may be concerned by the extra workload for the on-site sub contractors, additional hours will be shared out and therefore not place undue pressure on any one individual, and the EU Working Time Directives will still be followed.

In the longer term, D plc will be looking to speak to specialist agencies with a view to recruiting more skilled labour from overseas to avoid a repeat of this issue.

The HR Director will also investigate the possibility of setting up an apprenticeship scheme to enable D plc to develop its own workforce in the future – your thoughts on this would be much appreciated.

Kind regards

An Accountant

Exercise 2 - An e-mail with graph / chart attached

Email to the Board of D plc

To: Procurement Director
From: An Accountant
Date : Today
Subject : National supplier proposal

In advance of signing a long term contract it is recommended that a three-month trial period in the Central Region is entered into.

The trial period will allow D to test whether such an arrangement could work with our current IT system, as well as giving an opportunity to assess the quality and reliability of GreatBricks.

If the trial is successful, then a five-year deal should be agreed; this will result in £24m in savings per year.

This will also establish a long-term relationship to guarantee quality and timely supply of bricks in the future.

Not being able to supply Newco bricks restricts the benefits of using a sole supplier for the houses within the H brand, hopefully GreatBricks can remedy this situation.

Kind regards,

An Accountant

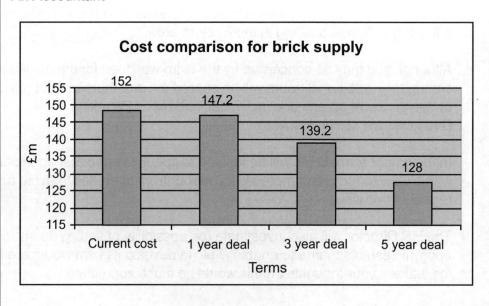

Exercise 3 - A letter

D plc
UK Head Office
Date (exam)

Sales Director Address

Dear Sales Director

It is with regret that we accept your resignation letter, though understand you must have taken all considerations into account when making your decision.

D plc places on record its thanks for your professionalism and commitment to making our company one of the best house-builders in the country.

You are reminded that your notice period is for three months from the resignation date, which we expect you to fulfil.

If there is no suitable internal candidate in the long term, then there is a possibility of external recruitment. It remains your responsibility to ensure a smooth handover regardless of which option occurs.

For any temporary replacement, you will be expected to work closely with them, getting them fully up to speed with your contacts and work practices. This co-ordination role will be of great importance to D plc to ensure our operations are not affected in any way.

D plc acknowledges that as you are going to a competitor, you are reminded of D plc's ethical code of conduct to ensure confidentiality of our business information remains.

In relation to this, as you may expect, you will be excluded from your Board meeting duties for D plc as of today.

If you have any concerns on the above, please do not hesitate to contact the Board immediately.

Yours sincerely,

D plc CEO

Exercise 4 - A presentation

Presentation to the Board

- H, R & S brands are well established in the market place
- Allows effective market segmentation
- Product appears tailored to needs of customer
- Helps with dream building
- Driven by marketing: consistent messages
- Extended through sales focused at site level
- Recommend marketing performed at regional level, sales still under brand executive
- Still enabling some local knowledge to form part of the marketing activity.
- More consistent message
- Less conflict due to regional control

Exercise 4 - A presentation